BACK TO MANDALAY

BURMESE LIFE, PAST AND PRESENT

GOLD SPONSORS

KAINNARIE

SILVER SPONSORS

 **FUJIFILM**

 Mitsubishi Corporation

SILKAIR

Summit Parkview
Yangon

BACK TO MANDALAY

BURMESE LIFE, PAST AND PRESENT

ABBEVILLE PRESS PUBLISHERS

NEW YORK   LONDON   PARIS

First published in the United States of America in 1996 by
Abbeville Press, 488 Madison Avenue, New York, N.Y. 10022.

First published in Great Britain in 1996
by Co & Bear Productions Ltd,
Richmond House, St Anne's Place, St Peter Port,
Guernsey GY1 3YS

Created by Co & Bear Productions (UK) Ltd.
Copyright ©1996 Co & Bear Productions Ltd.
Copyright ©1996 by Norman Lewis.

First Edition
10 9 8 7 6 5 4 3 2 1

ISBN 0-7892-0254-9

Printed in Italy by Officine Grafiche De Agostini, Novara
on Mitsubishi 5F-4/4 colour.

Editor *Gillian Cribbs*
Production editor *Laura Ivill*
Designers *Paul Ashby, Neil Newnum, Emma Skidmore*
Map illustrator *Andrew Farmer*
Picture assistant *David Shannon*
Publishers *Beatrice Vincenzini, Charles Orchard*

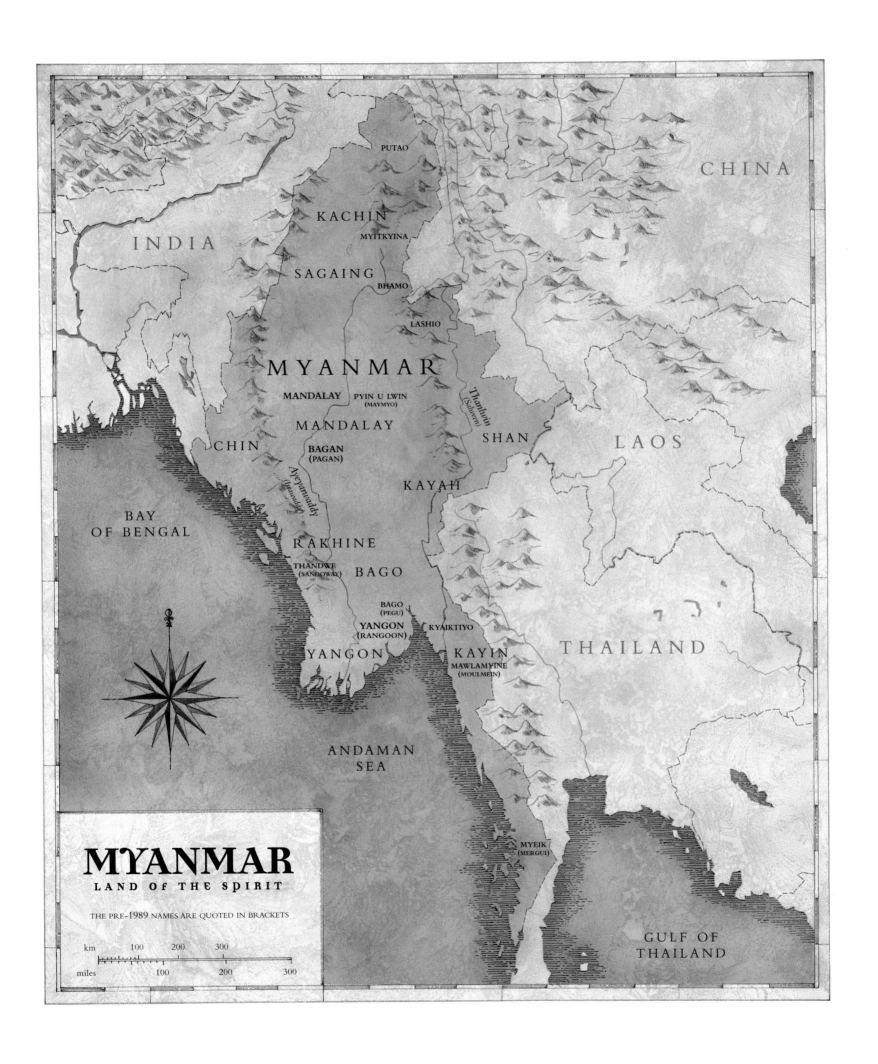

CHINA

PUTAO

KACHIN

MYITKYINA

INDIA

SAGAING

BHAMO

LASHIO

MYANMAR

MANDALAY   PYIN U LWIN
                (MAYMYO)

Thanlwin
(Salween)

MANDALAY

SHAN

LAOS

CHIN

BAGAN
(PAGAN)

Ayeyarwaddy
(Irrawaddy)

KAYAH

BAY
OF BENGAL

RAKHINE

THANDWE
(SANDOWAY)   BAGO

BAGO
(PEGU)

YANGON
(RANGOON)   KYAIKTIYO

THAILAND

YANGON   KAYIN

MAWLAMYINE
(MOULMEIN)

ANDAMAN
SEA

MYEIK
(MERGUI)

GULF OF
THAILAND

MYANMAR

LAND OF THE SPIRIT

THE PRE-1989 NAMES ARE QUOTED IN BRACKETS

km   100   200   300

miles   100   200   300

CONTENTS

CHAPTER ONE

MYIT~KYI AYE~YAR

Mighty Ayeyarwaddy

By Miranda Bruce-Mitford

'The Irrawaddy is of all the great rivers of Indochina the greatest…Its length and volume, its importance as an artery of the world, its rise and fall – these are easily recorded facts. The beauty of its waters that mirror a sky of varied loveliness, of its hills and forests and precipitous heights, of its vast spaces that bring calm to the most fretful spirit, of the sunsets that wrap it in mysteries of colour – these are things for which words are greatly inadequate.'

V C Scott O'Connor, The Silken East *(1904)*

Sunset falls over a small rowing boat gliding along the Ayeyarwaddy.

Passengers crowd onto a departing ferry in Yangon harbour.

WHEN RUDYARD KIPLING IMMORTALISED the Ayeyarwaddy River as 'the road to Mandalay', he was only stating what had been obvious to the people of Myanmar for thousands of years. Civilisations had developed along the banks of the great river for many centuries and before the advent of railways and cars the Ayeyarwaddy had provided the only important highway for commerce and travel in the country. Even today the majority of Myanmar's population still lives within a few miles of the river or a tributary navigable by small boat.

In fact, the Ayeyarwaddy, a great, lazy, sprawling river of more than 2,000 kilometres (navigable for 1,450 kilometres), runs way beyond Mandalay. It stretches from the source in the southern Himalayas, through the narrow gorge above Bhamo and down to the vast, humid delta where the river divides into eight main branches and finally flows into the Andaman Sea.

Only one bridge, the Ava bridge outside Mandalay, spans the Ayeyarwaddy. All other crossings are made by ferries or boats of all shapes and sizes, from lumbering paddle steamers and large ferries, to small boats and long, narrow rowing boats.

The Ayeyarwaddy developed into Myanmar's main commercial artery for largely practical reasons. During the monsoon season roads quickly develop potholes and become flooded and overgrown, bullock carts get stuck in the mud and lose their wheels, and drivers lose their tempers. Yet, even at the height of the dry season, the river is navigable as far north as Bhamo and, in the rainy season, further to Myitkyina. A ceaseless, silent flow of silt-laden water it is, sometimes dangerous to navigate it is true, but if one relies on experienced navigators the river becomes a peaceful, pleasurable way of travelling between one place and another.

According to the writer Sir J G Scott the Ayeyarwaddy's character dramatically changes as it winds through each of its three defiles, the first of which he describes as 'pleasing', the second as 'striking' and the third as 'savage'.

It was southwards down this great river valley that the early inhabitants of Myanmar descended from China and Tibet over many centuries. Traditional hill dwellers kept to high levels to the east and west and remained comparatively isolated, but the peoples who moved into the fertile valleys were to become the groups that shaped Myanmar's history: the Pyu, the Mons and later the Burmans, who established the Kingdom of Bagan in 1044 AD.

The early valley dwellers built their cities on the flat land and they cultivated soil that was fertile enough to support large populations. Major external influences permeated these civilisations from the coast by way of the river – Arab *dhows* and Chinese junks and, later, Portuguese galleons and Persian sailing ships, encouraging and enriching the development of the great city states – Sri Kshetra, Bagan, Sagaing, Ava, Amarapura and Mandalay. All were built in what is now called the dry zone of central Myanmar along the banks of the Ayeyarwaddy. Yangon lies on the Yangon River in the delta and is connected to the main Ayeyarwaddy by the Twantay Canal.

In a very real sense then, whoever controlled the river also controlled the country. However, it was not only in military terms that the Ayeyarwaddy figured: it was the lifeblood of the city state. Almost everything needed by the

A young worker inspects the molasses at a refinery, Lashio.

population was brought by river: rice, sugar cane, flour, vegetables and fruit to feed the population; cotton and textiles to clothe them; and bricks, lime, teak and bamboo for building. Labour, brought in to work on the construction of great temples and pagodas, and visiting embassies and soldiers were also transported by river.

The British discovered the necessity for river travel in the 19th century when they were involved in the Anglo-Burmese wars. They also understood the need to control the river and access to the sea. The small fleet of paddle steamers and shallow draft barges, or flats, which carried troops and supplies, was later sold as a commercial enterprise and the Irrawaddy Flotilla Company was formed in 1863.

At its height the company operated nearly 200 powered vessels, mostly paddle steamers, and more than 300 flats. These plied the river between Bhamo and Yangon carrying government officials, traders, passengers, mail and trade commodities such as rice. The time taken to complete such a journey depended on weather conditions. In the rainy season and immediately afterwards it took one week to travel from Yangon to Mandalay, a journey which lasted only a few days when the river was lower.

First-class travel on board a Company steamer was a comfortable experience then. There were individual cabins, a dining room, waiter service and bacon and eggs for breakfast. A whisky or Mandalay rum on deck at sunset was *de rigeur* for some. On the lower deck, however, conditions were somewhat different and much the same as those encountered on passenger steamers today.

These days, everyone is usually crammed together on deck. People unroll rush mats and perhaps a blanket, unpack tiffin boxes with cold rice and curry inside, and squat on their haunches to wait – for hours or days – until they reach their destination. There may be a cabin on board but it will hold seven or eight. Privacy is not an important consideration.

The boat pulls in from time to time at villages along the way, and an army of women and children descend on the steamer, all shouting at the tops of their voices for passengers to buy rice and curry, pancakes, sweetmeats and other foodstuffs. Occasionally there is also a canteen of sorts on board. I remember approaching the cooking area (an open fire on deck) and sensing an uneasy movement around it. Looking down I discovered to my horror that the deck had become alive with thousands of insects after food too – cockroaches.

However, the river is not only used by long-distance travellers. In the past, all the great cities of Myanmar had communities of river dwellers who lived in small houses of

Inle's famous floating market is held every five days at Ywama.

wood and bamboo along the banks and subsisted by fishing or unloading boats. Mandalay still has such houses, although fewer now than in the past. They stand quite close together on tall wooden stilts over the water. Access is by boat or narrow jetty and children here, as on Inle Lake, learn to swim very early in life. Houses are often a single room divided by a curtain with a verandah for cooking and a small fenced platform at the end of a narrow walkway where one can relieve oneself in deceptive privacy straight into the water a couple of metres below.

Drifting past, one feels like a voyeur glimpsing briefly into other people's lives, at once strange and familiar: families cooking, eating, arguing and defecating. We wave to each other, and a moment lights up briefly as the river sweeps us on to our destination.

Many villages stand beside the Ayeyarwaddy, each with its own pagoda gleaming white in the sun. The pagodas look peaceful from the river, but there is movement all along the banks. As with other great rivers of the world, such as the Ganges, Nile and Yangtze, fishermen can be seen casting their nets while small boys leap with yells and great splashes into the water, and water buffalo snort lazily with nostrils just protruding from the water. Women gather together to beat and scrub clothes in the shallows, then spread them out to dry while they wash themselves in the river, *longyis* tucked in above their breasts, scrubbing their bodies as vigorously as they scrub their clothes.

The farming community is closely bound to the vagaries of the river, whose waters bring valuable silt to the soil as they recede after the rainy season. The river's network of tributaries and canals irrigates vast tracts of land, used mostly to cultivate wet rice or paddy. Much of this rice finds its way into cities via the river and, in the past, when Myanmar was the world's leading rice exporter, it was subsequently shipped overseas.

Some villagers specialise in trades such as pottery, and these villagers send shipments of pots by river. Rafts laden with such wares are a familiar sight, as are the shipments of *ngapi*, the pungent fish used in Myanma cuisine.

Teak is still floated down river from the northern forested regions in the traditional way. It is dragged to the water by elephant, lashed together into great long rafts and drifted downstream by two or three men, who erect a little shelter on the raft and settle down for several weeks' travel. At their destination the logs are loosened and dragged ashore by patient water buffalo that manoeuvre it onto carts to be carried to saw mills nearby.

Myanmar is rich in oil, rubber, jute, zinc, tin and copper and is famous for its gems – jade, rubies, sapphires and cultivated pearls – which are sold every year at the Yangon Gem Emporium. Factories produce goods mainly for local consumption. The country's major exports are primary products such as rice and teak.

Railways were introduced to Myanmar in 1869, following the opening of the Suez Canal, to cope with the fast-growing export and import trade. By the end of the century, when the great Gokteik Viaduct was built on the Mandalay-Lashio branch, it was thought that there would be a rail link with China at the Kunlong Ferry and that Yangon would thus be an outlet to the sea for south-west China.

Since Myanmar had had water transport for centuries it was natural that the railways should be built to serve areas unreachable by river. The railways never run parallel to the Ayeyarwaddy for long stretches although they touch it at Henzada, Prome, Myingyan, Sagaing, Mandalay and Myitkyina. People do travel by rail, but trains are not always reliable and are much more expensive than the boats and steamers, which are always crammed with passengers.

Not unnaturally the river has become central to many of Myanmar's festivals. In the month of *Tawthalin* (August/September), when the river is in full spate, the boat-racing festival is held on lakes and rivers throughout the country. The banks of the Ayeyarwaddy are crowded as villagers and townsfolk watch the young men compete, and there is much noisy speculation about the races.

The festival most often associated with the river is *Thadingyat*, the festival of lights, which falls on the full moon of September/October. It is held to celebrate the descent of

Fishermen use traditional boats that are reminiscent of Arab dhows.

the Buddha from *Tavatimse* heaven, where he had gone to preach to his mother. At dusk people go down to the river's edge and place tiny candles onto leaf and twig rafts, which then float away on the current – a million pin-pricks of light illuminating the darkness – just as the celestials lit the Buddha's path as he descended to earth from heaven.

Myanma people are not a particularly romantic race; they tend to be rather down to earth and not given to writing poetry about the mighty Ayeyarwaddy. For them the river is simply an integral part of life. It has always been there and always will be there. It has been left to foreigners, entranced by its magic and mystique, to describe the river in their poems and prose. Of all the writers who have been captivated by the Ayeyarwaddy, none evoked its atmosphere better than Kipling in his poem *Mandalay*.

> *Come you back to Mandalay,*
> *Where the old Flotilla lay:*
> *Can't you 'ear their paddles chunkin' from Rangoon*
> *to Mandalay?*
> *On the road to Mandalay,*
> *Where the flyin'-fishes play,*
> *An' the dawn comes up like thunder outer China*
> *'crost the Bay!*

MIRANDA BRUCE-MITFORD *is tutor for Sotheby's Asian Arts course and is a guest lecturer for Swann Tours.*

9

PLANTING TIME

Country girls take a break from work in the fields. The work is
back-breaking, but a smile is never far from their faces.

EVENING COOL, MIDDAY SHADE

A buffalo boy returns from the fields at the end of a hard day and
a young woman is shaded by a bale of rice on her head.

11

PADDY NURSERY, AMARAPURA

Rice plants are transplanted for the dry-season crop. The rich plains of the central region around Mandalay are the 'rice bowl' of Myanmar.

13

GOODS FOR SALE
Fruit and vegetables, sweetmeats, cheroots and tea are in plentiful
supply in the markets of Maymyo, Myitkyina and Bhamo.

FLOATING MARKET, YWAMA, INLE LAKE (OVERLEAF)
Inle's famous floating market is held every five days and attracts
people from the 200 villages on and around the lake. Inle Lake
extends nearly 100 km north to south but is only 5 km wide.

16

ASPECTS OF AGRICULTURE

A village woman examines the cabbage crop, a family returns home
from the fields, and agricultural workers prepare to sell their wares.
Almost three-quarters of Myanmar's population are rural, and
agriculture supports two-thirds of the nation.

NAGA HUT NEAR THE CHINDWIN RIVER, KHANTI

*The traditional Naga house is built on poles; the hanging baskets store
chickens and small domestic animals.*

18

WORKING THE LAND

A procession of ox-drawn carts sets off from the village to market.
Buffalo and oxen still work the land in rural Myanmar, where
mechanised farming equipment is a rare sight.

PADDY THRESHERS

Two young boys begin the arduous task of separating rice from paddy
on the road to Bagan from Meiktila.

A FERTILE LAND
*Annual flooding and rich alluvial deposits make the soil in Myanmar's
southern delta region perfect for rice cultivation.*

RICE BOWL OF THE EAST
*'...we have seen the paddy sown out and mown, and passing from the
hands of the cultivators, through the mills, into the great ships that carry
the rice away to all parts of the world.'*
Shway Yoe, The Burman, His Life and Notions (1882)

FISHERMEN OF INLE LAKE

The Intha people of Inle Lake are well-known for their one-legged rowing technique, which the fishermen developed in order to keep two hands free for fishing.

MODERN WAYS
A fishing trawler in the Mergui Archipelago hauls in the nets.
Traditional and modern fishing methods exist side by side in Myanmar.

THE DAY'S CATCH
A Shan market stall in Maymyo displays the best of the day's catch.

SUNSET CALM
Fishermen return with their catch.

24

MEDICINAL ROOTS, BONES AND TALISMANS
A Shan trader selling traditional medicines and charms – bones, claws
and armadillo shells – at Maymyo market.

WAITING FOR A FARE

Bicycle trishaw drivers wait in rank for customers. Trishaws are a
popular form of transport in cities such as Yangon and Mandalay.

AT SUNDOWN
*In cloud glow at twilight
the beauty of the village swells
scent of mango and residual dew
consumes another cool season*
Nu Yin, The Gleaner *(1971)*

TRADITIONAL CRAFTS

*An old woman and her daughter spin cotton in Bhamo, as do the
'giraffe' women in a Padaung village. Candlemaking is another craft
continued by the women.*

29

BASKET WEAVING
Fixed in concentration a Palaung woman adds the finishing touches
to a woven basket in a village near Kalaw.

MORNING MARKET, KHANTI (OVERLEAF)
'The merchandise was foreign-looking, queer and poor. There were vast
pomelos…red bananas, baskets of heliotrope-coloured prawns…dried
fish, crimson chillis…green coconuts…Chinese sweetmeats… Elizabeth's
head was beginning to swim.'
George Orwell, Burmese Days *(1934)*

AVA BRIDGE AT SUNSET

The only bridge in Myanmar to cross the Ayeyarwaddy, the
1,198 kilometre-long Ava Bridge, was built by the British in 1934
and blown up by them in 1942 to halt the Japanese advance into
Myanmar. Ava Bridge was rebuilt and reopened in 1954 and, despite
its name, bypasses Ava, connecting Amarapura with Sagaing.

GOODS AND TRANSPORT

Hundreds of lacquer pots stacked on the banks of the Ayeyarwaddy.
Many local goods are dispatched to market by river on a sampan.

TWO FOR THE POT

Two young men carry a vast amphora along the banks of the
Ayeyarwaddy. A jar of this size would be used to store rice or water.

34

THROUGH THE CLOUDS

A village woman rakes and cools lime in a factory at Gau Win Ghat.

The lime is used to make building mortar and as a fertiliser for crops.

BUFFALO POINT, MANDALAY

A young woman and child deftly step across bamboo logs awaiting transportation by river to Yangon.

PARADISE ISLAND

Palm trees fringe the beautiful, unspoilt beaches of Banana Island, off the Tenasserim coast in the Andaman Sea.

TRANQUILLITY

Banana Island, picturesque yet remote, is consequently visited by very few tourists.

MYEIK COAST

Capital of Tenasserim Division, Myeik is also well known for its edible birds' nests.

NGAPALI BEACH (ARAKAN STATE)
'But in Rangoon the thoughts of the holidaymaker are not
always on Amhurst. Some romantic souls swear by a romantic spot
near Sandaway.'
W J Grant, The New Burma *(1940)*

CHAPTER TWO

BOK~DA BA~THA

Religion of the Buddha

By U Khin

'The Buddhist religion is perhaps the least gloomy of all those creeds which involve a belief in the immortality of the soul. There is no eternity of hell; no hopeless state of damnation even for the worst of criminals. The soul may be condemned to a lower state of existence in the next life, or even to a limited hell; but existence is practically eternal until, by many lives of purity and contemplation, the spirit sinks into the beatified repose of nirvana.'

J T Wheeler, Journal of a Voyage up the Irrawaddy *(1871)*

The great central terrace of the Shwedagon pagoda, Yangon.

Two young novice monks enjoy a cool refreshing drink at a roadside stall.

THE VERY FIRST SIGHTS A VISITOR NOTICES as he or she flies over Myanmar are the myriad white pagodas that dot the landscape. Some stand on hilltops, some on riverbanks, while others hold commanding positions in villages and towns. All of these pagodas, from the smallest village temple to the mighty Shwedagon in Yangon, stand as testimony to the piety and generosity of the people, and reveal the depth of their Buddhist faith.

Pagodas in Myanmar are beautifully maintained, and families spend much of their hard-earned income on donations for their upkeep. This, together with simple acts of charity, such as feeding the monks and applying gold leaf to Buddha images, earn them *kusala* (merit) in this life and the chance to progress to a higher form of existence in future lives. They also spend considerable sums on pilgrimages to pagodas throughout the country for the many Buddhist festivals throughout the year.

The monastery, traditionally the centre for education, is still the focal point of every village. Monks are respected as community leaders and act as healers, councillors and teachers. They occupy the highest position in Myanmar's social hierarchy. Nuns are not ordained, and few women in Myanmar choose to follow a religious life. Although monks are regularly fed, as donations earn merit, nuns must beg for money and do not hold such a respected place in society.

The vast majority (around 85 per cent) of Myanma people are devout Buddhists. Buddhism is in every way a living religion in Myanmar. It brings solace in times of sorrow, inspiration in times of dejection and deep contentment in times of happiness. It offers security, satisfaction and general well-being in the present, and promises a better life in the hereafter – in all future lives until *Nirvana*, the ultimate bliss.

It is generally accepted that Theravada Buddhism came to Myanmar as early as the 4th and 5th century AD although it did not become established there until the 11th century. The religion was introduced by Indian traders, adventurers and immigrants who also taught a variety of other religious cults, including Mahayanist and Tantric Buddhism and

Vishnuism. One of the main cults in existence when Theravada Buddhism took root was a Varjrayana-type of Buddhism mixed with animistic beliefs, which was run by the Aris, an order of corrupt monks. King Anawrahta of Bagan stamped out this cult when he came to the throne in 1044 AD and established Theravada Buddhism in its place with the help of Shin Arahan, a Mon monk from Thaton in Lower Burma. Anawrahta also acquired the Buddhist Pali canon, originally from Sri Lanka, which he introduced to his people.

Anawrahta tolerated *nat* (spirit) worship in pagoda precincts in an attempt to fuse Buddhism with pre-Buddhist animism. This tradition survives today; modern Buddhists are still conscientious enough to visit *nat* ceremonies and appease the spirits at shrines near the pagoda.

The people of Myanmar are descendants of Tibeto-Burman tribes who once occupied the plateaux of Central Asia. On their migratory movements south across towering hills, arid deserts and dense forests, they became hardy, brave warriors. When they reached the Ayeyarwaddy Valley they discovered a hospitable land with a temperate climate and fertile soil. They quickly occupied the region, built villages and towns and worked the land; when rainfall was scant, they built irrigation canals and dams.

Under Theravada Buddhism these hardy warriors began to pursue a peaceful way of life and after a while became quite gentle. They tried to fulfil, as best they could, the three fundamental duties of all Buddhists: *dana* (charity), *sila* (ethical conduct) and *bhavana* (mental discipline or meditation). Even if they could not fulfil the duties of *sila* and *bhavana* all the time, they would spare no effort to perform *dana* – so much so that the generosity of these people became legendary.

Soon they became very enthusiastic about religion. Led by their kings they began to build pagodas at Bagan of such magnificence and beauty that pagodas such as the Shwezigon, Ananda and Thatbyinnyu are rightly recognised today as breathtaking works of art and architecture. Legend has it that Bagan once boasted more than four million

Statue of the Buddha inside the Dhammayangyi temple, Bagan.

pagodas although many were destroyed when Kublai Khan, the Mongol leader, and his Tartar hordes invaded in 1287 AD. Nevertheless, there are still more than 4,000 stupas, Buddhist shrines, left standing in Bagan in an area measuring just 41 square kilometres.

Today, devotees of Buddhism acknowledge the Buddha, the *dhamma* (his teaching) and *sangha* (brotherhood of monks), known as the *tri ratana* (triple gem). As Buddhists they must observe five precepts: they must refrain from killing, stealing, sexual misconduct, telling falsehoods and taking drugs or other intoxicants. These precepts are the minimum obligatory undertaking for every Buddhist.

The first daily duty of the Buddhist is to acknowledge the *tri ratana* three times in Pali. The next step is to declare that he undertakes the five precepts, followed by the offering of *hsoon* (usually cooked rice and fruit), water, flowers and incense at a statue of the Buddha. This is done in piety and gratitude to the Buddha for his teachings. After the offerings the devotee will announce that he is sharing his meritorious deeds with all beings, in the human, celestial and nether realms.

Some Buddhists also recite the 11 *suttas*, special discourses of Buddha that they believe have protective power against harm and danger. The ones on the 38 blessings and *metta* (loving kindness) are extremely popular and many young children know them by heart. More serious Buddhists will recite the law of dependent origination, or

41

conditioned genesis (*patissa samuppada*). According to this law nothing in the mundane world is absolute: everything is conditioned, relative and interdependent. The doctrine of *anatta* (without ego) becomes more understandable when studied in the light of *patissa samuppada*.

However, the duties of a Buddhist are not only to observe *sila*, give *dana* and practise *bhavana*. The buddhist is also expected to allow his son to become a novice monk so that the boy will have some experience of monastic life. This is known as *Shinbyu* and is one of the most important tasks a Buddhist can perform. The boy may only wear the robe for a week or a fortnight, but the ceremony is considered the most important day in his life and the most meritorious deed his parents can perform in their lifetimes.

'A Burmese boy is not considered to be a good Buddhist until he has gone through this religious rite of initiation; and a Burmese adult does not attain the status of gentleman until he has sponsored such a ceremony…it is counted as the highest spiritual and ethical performance to posterity, for which both the parents and the son achieve immense merit in this world and the hereafter.

This explains why the birth of a son in a Buddhist family is cordially welcomed and hailed with great rejoicing.'

Sao Htun Hmat Win,
Initiation of Novicehood and Ordination of
Monkhood in Burmese Buddhist Culture *(1986)*

The time and date of the Shinbyu is fixed by astrologers and the young boy is dressed in the finest clothes and jewels his family can borrow or buy. He is paraded on a throne seated on a horse or elephant as the villagers feast in celebration. Later he is led to the monastery where the abbot divests him of his robes and jewels and shaves his head, while his close relatives look on and say prayers. The young boy then puts on the yellow robes of the monk, and joins the monastery as a novice.

The *Shinbyu* ceremony represents the story of Prince Siddhartha, a young prince of the Sakya tribe of Nepal, who later became Gautama, the Buddha, as recorded in the Jataka tales. During his early years Siddhartha was shielded from the harsher side of life by his father but during his travels he came across four things – a helpless old man, a sick man, a corpse and a beggar – which made him renounce his princely life and follow the path to enlightenment. Dressed as a prince, the young boy represents the young Gautama whereas the removal of his fine clothes and jewels and the shaving of his head symbolise the Buddha's renunciation of worldly pleasures.

At the heart of Buddhist teaching lie the four noble Truths enunciated by the Buddha in his first sermon at the deer park in Sarnath near India's holy city of Benares. The first noble Truth, according to the Buddha, is that life is subject to *dukkha* (suffering): impermanence, imperfection, and unsatisfactoriness are universal laws, therefore life itself is suffering. The second Truth is that suffering is caused by clinging to and craving sensual pleasures and thirsting for existence which is due to ignorance. The third Truth is the ultimate cessation of *dukkha*, which is known as *Nibbanna* in Pali and *Nirvana* in Sanskrit. Ordinary mundane words

A Shinbyu procession en route to the monastery. The abbot awaits the young prince.

42

cannot describe *Nirvana*, which Buddhists recognise as a supra-mundane state of existence. It is the state of supreme bliss, freed from all attachment and thirst for rebirth.

> *'Give up the past, give up the future, give up the present. Having reached the end of existence, with a mind freed from all [conditioned things], you will not again undergo birth and decay.'*
>
> Ugasena Vatthu

Finally comes the fourth noble Truth, the *magga* (path) to eliminate desires, which leads to attaining *Nirvana*.

However, for ordinary people the three words from the scriptures that seem to sum up their devotion are: *anicca* (impermanence), *dukkha* (suffering) and *anatta* (no self, no soul, no ego). They will utter these words when they count their prayer beads, when they meditate and when they attend a funeral. When someone dies people will say: 'So and So has reached the state of *anicca*!' These three words describe the nature of existence for Buddhists: *anicca* is quite obvious, as nothing in this world is permanent and *dukkha*, as explained by the Buddha in his first sermon, is corollary to *anicca*. However, *anatta* is unique to Buddhism. According to *anatta* there is no permanent entity in humans that can be called a self or soul: man is made up of fine aggregates – or *skandas* – such as the body, feelings, perceptions, impulses emotions and consciousness. When a person dies there is no soul to reincarnate, as there is nothing permanent that can leave the body and enter another.

Myanma people are not overly concerned with the concept of *dukkha*, although they are fully aware of it. They know they can be released from suffering by following the Middle Way, also known as the Noble Eightfold Path. For this they must follow eight requirements namely: right understanding, thought, speech, action, livelihood, effort, mindfulness and concentration.

Knowing there is an antidote to suffering, Myanma people have a generally optimistic outlook on life. They will therefore happily give away money to charity, contribute to

A shaft of sunlight picks out a devotee at prayer inside the Baukyo pagoda.

the building of pagodas, monasteries, and rest houses (*zayats*) for weary travellers, and pay for lavish festivals. Such is the life of the ordinary Buddhist. At pagoda festivals, monasteries, *Shinbyu* ceremonies and funerals they will discuss Buddhism in general terms, based on the concepts *anicca*, *dukkha*, *anatta* and *Nirvana*.

The majority of people will pray to reach 'the golden realm' of *Nirvana,* which will in turn bring them release from *karma*. Throughout their earthly life they will try to gain *kusala* (merit) by observing *sila* (following the five precepts or, if they are more serious Buddhists, the eight precepts and ten precepts), do as much charitable work (*dana*) as they can, and spend some time at the occasional meditation retreat (*bhavana*).

Many will pay for a *Shinbyu* for their sons or grandsons and some may themselves don the yellow robes of a monk for a few days. However, most will leave the life of the homeless *bikkhu* (monk) to those who have renounced the world and have chosen a life governed by the ten precepts and 227 rules of monastery.

For the most part the ordinary Myanma Buddhist will be content to live in the mundane world – happy, generous and occasionally contemplative.

U KHIN, *a retired director of information for the Myanma Government and broadcaster for BBC World Service, gives regular lectures on Buddhism at the Britain-Burma Society.*

43

44

A TRUSTED FRIEND

'Health is the greatest gift, contentment is the greatest wealth,
a trusted friend is the greatest relative.'
Pasenadikosala Vatthu

SILENT CONTEMPLATION
'Fully alert and ever vigilant are Gautama Buddha's disciples, whose minds by day and night cultivate goodwill towards everyone.'
Darusakatikaputta Vatthu

MORNING STUDIES
Young monks in Yangon and nuns in Sagaing pore over the Buddhist scriptures, the Triptaka (Three Baskets). The texts are written in Pali, an ancient Indian language.

SHINBYU CEREMONY

'The prince boy (Shin laung) dressed in Royal costume stays in a
decorated pandal, seated on a glittering chaise. The pandal is symbolic
of a palace and the seat a throne. The prince is enjoying worldly
pleasures in a Royal house prior to his deliberate denunciation of the
world to become a novice or a recluse.'
Sao Htun Hmat Win, Initiation of Novicehood (1986)

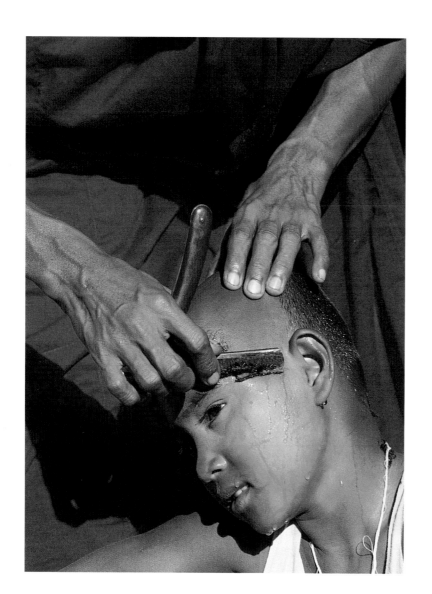

48

INITIATION

After the Shinbyu, the abbot shaves the neophyte's head before he dons the yellow robes and enters the monastery.

WATCHFULNESS

Young neophytes observing a Shinbyu ceremony in Wap Win village. There is no lower age limit for young noviciates.

51

LIGHT AND SHADE
Monks use their fans to good effect as they venture into the village in
the heat of the day.

MIGHTY BUDDHA

A solitary monk prays before a reclining Buddha. This attitude represents Buddha's attainment of 'the point of final liberation'.

GOLDEN HANDS

Three monks contemplate their monastic life while the golden hands of Buddha at the Kabe Aye pagoda point downwards to earth and upwards to the heavens.

AN ACT OF MERIT

Pilgrims apply precious gold leaf to the famous statue of Buddha at Mandalay's Mahamuni pagoda.

SERENITY

'Him I call a brahmana, who, like the moon is pure, clear and serene
and in whom craving for existence is extinct.'
Candabhatthera Vatthu

BUDDHA'S TROVE

Many thousands of images of Buddha stand in the Pindaya Caves
near Aungban. The caves house a 12th-century stupa and several small
meditation chambers.

LORD OF THE PAGODAS (PREVIOUS PAGE)

The imposing figure of Gautama silently watches over the town of
Kyatpyin, north Mogok, upper Myanmar.

SHWEDAGON PAGODA

The golden stupa of the Shwedagon dominates Yangon and acts as a
spiritual magnet to Buddhist pilgrims throughout Myanmar and
Indo-China. It was originally built around 600 BC to house eight
sacred hairs of the Buddha.

SHWEDAGON PAYA

*'Of all the shrines, the Shwedagon, the most venerable place of worship
in all the Indo-Chinese countries, is the most universally visited.'*
Shway Yoe, The Burman, His Life and Notions *(1882)*

THE NOBLE ORDER

'Let his life be kindness, his conduct righteousness; then in the fullness
of gladness he will make an end of grief.'
Dammapada

63

BEHIND THE BAMBOO CURTAIN
The face of Buddha gazes out through a mesh of bamboo erected for restoration work.

TEMPLE HOSTS
Hundreds of carved stone figures adorn the walls of the Sri Kaliyamman temple in Yangon.

KYAIKTIYO PAGODA

'A few hours' journey from Pegu is the little town of Kyaikto with its
balancing pagoda of Kyaiktiyo which is built on the top of a boulder
balanced on the edge of a precipice, and is more wonderful even than
the leaning Tower of Pisa.'
F Haskings (1944)

THE GOLDEN ROCK

Kyaiktiyo is an ancient Mon-Sanskrit name meaning 'pagoda
shouldered on the head of a hermit'. Pilgrims travel to worship at the
base of the 900-year-old Golden Rock with its balancing pagoda.

MORNING LIGHT

A monk enjoys the streaming sunlight in the Nga Hpe Chaung Monastery, Inle Lake.

WINDOW ON THE WORLD

Hopeful young novices gaze out from a carved window of the famous Teak Monastery, Inle Lake.

SOLITARY CONTEMPLATION

A young monk, deep in thought, is framed by one of the carved arches
in the Teak Monastery, Inle Lake.

SHWEZIGON PAGODA

A novice monk stands by an entrance to the ancient pagoda, Bagan,
built in 1089.

BUDDHA'S GIFTS

A woman makes an offering of flowers to the Dhammayangyi temple Buddha, Bagan. Flowers, incense and food are the usual offerings.

GILDED GLORY

Teak Buddha decorated with gold leaf at the Ananda temple, Bagan.

The temple houses 1,424 statues of Buddha.

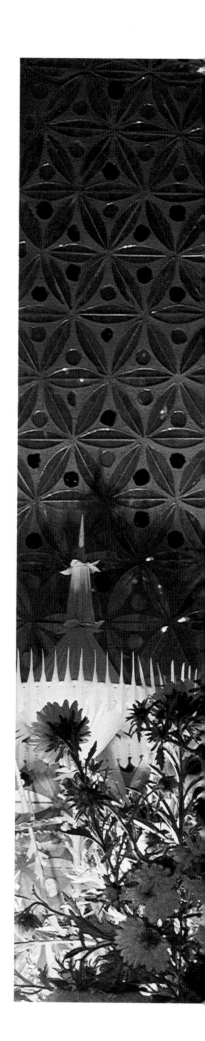

PEACE THROUGH PRAYER
'Not to do evil, to cultivate merit, to purify one's mind – this is the
teaching of the Buddhas.'
Anandattherapanha Vatthu

MYONAN PAGODA BUDDHA, LOIKAW
'Give up the past, give up the future, give up the present. Having
reached the end of existences, with a mind freed from everything, you
will not again undergo birth and decay.'
Ugasena Vatthu

CHAPTER THREE

BAGAN PYI
Kingdom of Bagan

By Professor Michael Aung-Thwin

'As we near Yenan-gyat there becomes visible, for the first time, the countless pyramids and spires of Pagan, the most stately capital Burma has ever known. The nearer ones are cut in dark outlines against the sky; the most distant are so faint that they seem like the unreal fabrics of a city of dreams. Yet there is nothing in this superb picture, in all these hosts of pinnacles and domes and spires, to hint that before one there lies a city of the dead.'

V C Scott O'Connor, The Silken East *(1904)*

King Bodawpaya's pagoda, Mingun, was split by an earthquake in 1838.

Bagan's many temples and pagodas emerge as the morning mist clears.

MYANMAR'S POLITICAL AND CULTURAL history has been largely shaped by its geography. Spanning 676,577 square kilometres, roughly the size of Texas, Myanmar's major mountain chains, the Arakan, Bago and Shan Yoma lie north-south, and its rivers, the Ayeyarwaddy, Chindwin, Sittang and Salween run more or less parallel. Myanmar is thus divided into long plains easily accessible from the north-south but difficult when moving east-west.

Historically the dry zone of the middle plains – the Ayeyarwaddy River Valley – has been Myanmar's political and cultural centre. Several cultural groups dominated this region. First came the Pyu, dominant during the last several centuries of the first millennium BC until the 9th century AD. The Burmans followed, holding power either in alliance, or in competition, with Myanmar's other two main ethnic groups, the Mons and Shans.

Although little archaeological work has been conducted in Myanmar, a palaeolithic and earlier neolithic period (around 11000 BC) seems to have been followed by an urbanised period of city-states around 200 BC. This was the Pyu period, which sowed the seeds for the Kingdom of Bagan in the mid-9th century AD. In turn, Bagan's traditions became the standard for Myanma society.

The political dominance of Bagan waned in the late 13th century as several centres of power competed for supremacy. By the second half of the late 14th century another dynasty modelled on Bagan was established, created by descendants of the old royal family. Their capital was Ava, which was situated approximately 128 kilometres north-east of Bagan.

Ava dominated the dry zone for 163 years, hemmed in to the north by the Shan, and by two other powers, Bago almost on the coast, and Toungoo further south of the dry zone. By the mid-16th century Toungoo's leaders had recaptured the Ayeyarwaddy River Valley, Ava and Bago, and had established their own dynasty. Less than 40 years later the centre of power had shifted back to Ava, which was revived as a capital and remained so until 1752 when it fell to Bago's forces.

However, Bago's bid for political domination was short-lived: a few months later its forces were driven from Ava and a new dynasty – the Konbaung – was formed by King Alaunghpaya. The Konbaung ruled until the 19th century when, after three wars (1824, 1852 and 1885-6), Britain took over. Only then did Yangon become the capital for administrative purposes.

Myanmar remained under British colonial rule until 1942 when the Japanese arrived. The Allied Forces retook control in 1944, but Myanmar won its independence in 1948. With Yangon as capital, the nation experimented with parliamentary democracy, socialism and federalism until, in 1962, it became a one-party socialist state. Although still a socialist state (albeit rapidly opening up to commerce) the survival of certain Myanma institutions, such as Theravada Buddhism and the *sangha* (order of monks), suggests that some of the changes in the last 100 years are not as profound as the continuities.

Under the PYU (2nd century BC to 9th century AD) Myanmar entered its formative period. A dozen brick-walled cities have been discovered, most in the dry zone. They were of a uniform culture and the inhabitants were probably a Tibeto-Burman speaking people. Three cities served successively as capitals during the Pyu period: Beikthano Myo, Hanlan and Sri Ksetra.

BEIKTHANO MYO, the earliest, was located in the dry zone. Its remains – structures, pottery, artefacts and human skeletons – date from 200 BC to 100 AD. Fortifications and rectangular city walls over three kilometres long on each side and about six metres thick have been found. Like most subsequent cities the main entrance led to the palace, which faced east. Stupas and monastic buildings have also been excavated within the city walls.

HANLAN (Halin) was located east of the Mu River, (now Shwebo district) in an area continuously inhabited from the 2nd to 3rd centuries AD. The city was rectangular and, like other Pyu cities, brick-walled. A river or canal ran through the city and a moat appears to have existed on three sides. There were 12 gateways exactly like those of 19th-century Mandalay. Structural remains show similarities with Beikthano, particularly the temples, which are also echoed in Bagan.

SRI KSETRA ('Field of Glory'), 240 kilometres from the sea near present-day Pyay, was the last and southernmost Pyu capital. It was probably founded in 638 AD and lasted until the 9th century. Circular in design, it was more than 13 kilometres in circumference and three to four kilometres across. Brick walls remain reaching a height of 4.5 metres, with huge *devas* (deities) or *bodhisattvas* guarding the entrances. There is evidence of a palace within the city walls, but most of the remaining monuments are stupas resembling styles found in later Bagan.

It is uncertain how the Pyu Kingdom ended, but a political vacuum was created in the mid-9th century which the Burmans subsequently filled.

BAGAN (Arimaddana Pura) was founded around 849 AD on the east bank of the Ayeyarwaddy. The choice was apparently strategic for it allowed Bagan's rulers to straddle the fertile plains of Upper Myanmar, stay far enough from the north (and invaders) and move quickly down river to control the coastal cities if needed.

What remains of the walled city suggests the usual configuration of a square with four main gates, the front

The thousands of temples on Bagan's plain are surrounded by mountains.

facing east, flanked on both sides by *nat* (spirit) shrines. What is important about Bagan is that, although the king's palace and some temples lay within the city of around two square kilometres, most of the temples, monasteries and rice lands lay outside the walls.

Pyu cities, in contrast with Bagan, are much larger – about 14 kilometres in circumference – which suggests that the Pyu lived within the walls. Bagan, it seems, was able to defend itself and a population living outside its walls. It was, therefore, more centralised – administratively, economically, and militarily – than Sri Ksetra.

From the Pyu period onwards, the symbolism of Myanmar's capitals (except Bago) was strikingly similar. The *myo* (city) had seven requisites: the proper arrangement of gates and ramparts, a moat, a royal pagoda, a royal ordination hall (*sima*), a royal monastery, a royal library and a royal preaching hall (*dhammasala*). Most cities had 12 gates – four at the cardinal points flanked by two intermediate gates. Mandalay, built 1,000 years later, reflected this 12-gate plan.

Inwa ('Replete with Power'), known in English as AVA, was later named Ratanapura ('City of Gems'). It lay at the junction of the Ayeyarwaddy and Myitnge Rivers,

The Dhammayangyi temple, built in 1167 AD, is the largest in Bagan.

128 kilometres north-east of Bagan. Ava was capital at least three times, so its original plan is not known but, like Bagan, its site had political and military significance.

Ava's east gate was located on the mouth of the Myitnge River where it debouched into the Ayeyarwaddy. This allowed Ava to control the Kyaukse plains, the granary of Upper Myanmar. Protected to the north by the Ayeyarwaddy, east by the Myitnge and south and west by a canal linking both rivers, Ava was, in fact, an island. In 1527 Ava was sacked by Thohanbwa, a Shan chieftain, and the royal family, monks and people fled south to Toungoo.

The Toungoo Dynasty differed from others in that it was the first and last to be situated near the coast. Refugees from Ava enabled Toungoo to expand under King Tabinshwehti and, in 1551, capture BAGO (Pakyu). The next king, Bayinnaung, made Bago his capital in 1553.

Bago was square but had a projection to the east where the older city, Pakyu, had been absorbed. The Bago River ran past its west wall providing a double moat. The new city and palace, rebuilt in 1564, followed the usual plan, with a few significant differences. First, the palace, great hall and Lion throne faced west rather than east. Second, Bago did not have 12 gates named after signs of the zodiac but 20 named after cities the king had conquered. Bayinnaung's innovations did not become tradition; by the end of the 16th century the remnants of the Burmese royal family had returned to the dry zone to resurrect Ava.

The royal family returned to Nyaungyan, Meiktila, a provincial centre in Upper Myanmar, where Bayinnaung's son, Nyaungyan Min, was governor. When Bago fell in 1597 refugees swelled Nyaungyan's army, and he took Ava, founding the Second Ava Dynasty. In 1600, after rebuilding the older city, Nyaungyan was crowned king.

AVA II (Inwa II) and its brick fortifications were square. A rectangular palace lay at the north-east corner of the city in a strong position at the confluence of the Ayeyarwaddy and Myitnge Rivers. It had the usual 12 gates.

The Second Ava Dynasty fell to Bago in 1752. King Mahadhammayazadipati and his family were transported to

Bago, and Dalaban ('Capturer of Dala') was made governor. He was soon challenged by Aung Zeya, a former tax collector, who had begun to fortify nearby SHWEBO.

Aung Zeya advanced down river from the Mu Valley and secured the lower Chindwin region. A charismatic leader, he attracted refugees who were given rice, clothing, arms and land. Officials familiar with state rituals also rallied to him, and on 21 June 1753, a propitious date, he constructed a capital, Yadana Theinga Konbaung Pran ('Kingdom of Konbaung, the Jewelled Lion'). Since he was not royal, Aung Zeya invented a genealogy tracing his lineage to Bagan and Pyusawthi, and was crowned King Alaunghpaya. He captured Ava on 3 January 1754, and proceeded to found a new dynasty.

When he died in 1760, Alaunghpaya left explicit orders for succession – reinforcing a principle from the Bagan period – which endured until 1782 when Prince Badon ousted his elder brother, Hsinhpyushin.

Prince Badon, later known as Bodawhpaya, built a new capital at AMARAPURA ('City of Immortals'). The city was a perfect square, with the usual 12 gates, one major gate on each side flanked by two intermediate gates. Like all royal cities Amarapura was moated and its banks lined with bricks. Only the four pagodas of the inner fort surrounding the palace remain today.

Bagyidaw, Bodawhpaya's grandson, moved his palace back to Ava in 1823, although his successor, King Tharawaddy (1837-56), moved it back to Amarapura, where it remained until King Mindon dismantled the palace and rebuilt it in Mandalay.

MANDALAY ('Magical Diagram') incorporated all the physical and symbolic components of earlier capitals, but it also reflected the 12-gate plan of Pyu cities. Each gate had a pillar bearing a sign of the zodiac, which was meant to signify cosmic time. Mandalay also represented cosmic space and power as it was modelled on mythical *Tavatimsa* – Buddhist heaven – where Sakra resided with 32 subordinate lords and four guardians of the world. The total of 37 is represented by 37 *pyathat* (towers) in the walled city, the

Many golden pagodas are lit by night so they dazzle as much as by day.

tallest over the Lion throne. In Buddhist cosmology this tower was supposed to be Mount Meru, a mountain on the southern island of Jambudipa, where *cakravartins* (world conquerors) are born and to which Maitreya, the future Buddha, will return.

The design and structure of the palace, at the centre of the city, was virtually identical to its precursors. Its nine thrones are located strategically; it has the Great Hall of Audience with the Lion throne in the east; some of the western apartments are reserved for the queens and members of the royal family, others are for important ministers of state.

Dagon was a small port city in the Bagan period and mentioned in 12th-century Old Burmese inscriptions. Renamed YANGON ('End of Enmity') by King Alaunghpaya in the 18th century after he had pacified the Ayeyarwaddy Delta, Yangon was later anglicised as Rangoon under British colonial rulers. Chosen for administrative and economic reasons, Yangon was not planned in the same way as pre-colonial capitals, nor did it represent the Buddhist cosmos like Mandalay. But it does reflect some features of its ancient predecessors, such as temples, royal gardens, monasteries and barracks for the king's troops.

MICHAEL AUNG-THWIN *is professor of South-East Asian Studies at the University of Hawaii at Manoa. His publications include 'Pagan, The Origins of Modern Burma' (1985).*

MAJESTIC ANANDA

Built by Bagan's founder, King Kyanzittha in 1091 AD, the Ananda temple is a masterpiece of Mon architecture and is the most venerated temple in Bagan. It symbolises the endless wisdom (Ananta Panna) of the Buddha.

MORNING MIST (OVERLEAF)

'Pagan, in many respects, is the most remarkable religious city in the world. Jerusalem, Rome, Benares...none of them can boast the multitude of temples...the lavishness of design and ornament.'
Shway Yoe, The Burman, His Life and Notions *(1882)*

INTRICATE CRAFT
*Wood carvings of gods and heroes engraved inside an archway of one
of Bagan's old monasteries.*

SULAMANI TEMPLE
*Elaborate stucco work in one of the entrances to the Sulamani temple.
Built by King Narapatisthu (1174-1211), it is an early example of
Bagan's Late Period.*

PEACE WITHIN
Buddha's serene image gazing down inside the Dhammayangyi temple, Bagan.

DHAMMAYANGYI TEMPLE
Built c1170 by King Narathu, who murdered his father and elder brother to seize the crown, Bagan's largest shrine was constructed as an act of atonement for the king's heinous crimes.

SUNSET ACROSS BAGAN'S PLAINS

The magnificent Thatbyinnyu temple (c1144) stands within the old city wall. Looking out from the top, thousands of temples can be seen adorning the plains.

88

ROYAL PALACE, GOLDEN TEMPLE

Shwegugyi, the Golden Cave temple, built in 1131 by King
Alaungsithu, stands beside the remains of the Royal Palace.

SHWESANDAW PAGODA

Built by King Anawrahta after his conquest of Thaton in 1057,
Shwesandaw pagoda is said to enshrine sacred hairs of the Buddha.

SUNRISE OVER SHWESANDAW

The stupa, silhouetted here at sunrise, shows a strong Mon influence. Long flights of steps lead up to the temple's five receding terraces which offer spectacular views over Bagan's plains. It is also known as the Ganesh pagoda because a stone figure of the elephant-god, Ganesh, was originally placed at each corner of the stone terraces.

UNQUESTIONED POWER (ABOVE AND OVERLEAF)
'The walled city...expanded far beyond its original defences and its
security, was felt to be unquestionable...Pagan in those days was
entitled Arimaddanapura, "the city that tramples down its foes".'
A B Griswold, Burma, Korea, Tibet (1940)

ON THE GREAT RIVER'S BANKS

*'…it looks, hung between the drowsy clouds and the mirror-like calm
of the mighty river, like some new Venice of the East, destined to play
an immortal part in the history of the world.'*
V C Scott O'Connor, The Silken East *(1904)*

ANCIENT WONDER

*Between the 11th and 13th centuries, 13,000 temples, pagodas and
monasteries were built on the plains of Bagan, of which 2,217 remain.*

UNIVERSAL SPLENDOUR
The Great Audience Hall, with its seven-tiered golden spire, stood at the 'centre of the universe' in Brahmin-Buddhist cosmology.

ROYAL PALACE, MANDALAY
The elaborate carvings of the Great Audience Hall and walls of the Royal Palace are the work of modern-day craftsmen who have painstakingly reconstructed Mandalay's most famous landmark that was built in 1857 by King Mindon and destroyed by fire in 1945.

THE WORLD'S LARGEST BOOK

A lone monk wanders through the Kuthodaw pagoda, Mandalay,
home to 729 marble tablets inscribed with the entire Buddhist canon.
A team of 2,400 monks worked on the book.

PATODAWGI PAGODA, AMARAPURA

Built by King Pagan Min in 1847 and modelled on the Ananda
pagoda, Bagan, the Patodawgi pagoda once marked the edge of
the ancient capital.

MANDALAY AT SUNDOWN
A boat puts in at a jetty on the Ayeyarwaddy River while sunset throws the Royal Palace's distinctive reflection into sharp relief.

102

LIGHT WITHIN
A brick statue of Buddha in the sanctuary of the Abeyadana temple.
The temple was named after the wife of its founder, King Kyanzittha.

MURAL, SULAMANI TEMPLE
The walls and vaults of the temple were originally covered with
murals. Those remaining date from the 18th century.

INNER SANCTUM

One of the eight statues of Buddha inside the Htilominlo temple, built c1211 by King Nadaungmya to commemorate the spot where he was chosen as crown prince.

STREET LIFE

Traffic squeezes along a busy Yangon road and people crowd the
pavements, but the narrow back streets are almost deserted.

YANGON WINDOWS

Most houses have wooden shutters to block out the fierce midday sun
and allow cool breezes to circulate at night.

SECRETARIAT BUILDING, YANGON

*This government office is another fine example of 19th-century
colonial architecture.*

BANK OF MYANMAR

The bank takes pride of place on Strand Road, the most famous
street in Yangon.

GOVERNMENT BUILDING, YANGON

*Fine examples of colonial architecture are common on Yangon's
Strand Road.*

111

TSING CHONG PALACE

Myanmar's Ministry of Culture is based in the former Tsing Chong Palace in Yangon.

COLONIAL GRANDEUR
British administrators of the 19th century built many imposing houses in the colonial style in Yangon.

ARCHITECTURAL SPLENDOUR

*Offices in Yangon are housed in some of the finest examples of
19th-century architecture in Asia.*

CLASSICAL STYLE

*Moulmein boasts some of the grandest buildings in Myanmar outside
the capital, Yangon.*

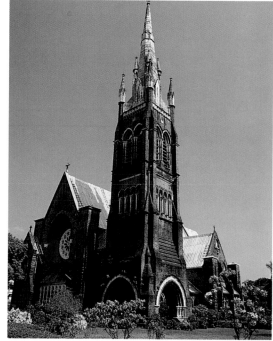

YANGON CENTRAL RAILWAY STATION
The capital's main terminal is modelled on 19th-century English railway stations.

ANGLICAN CATHEDRAL, YANGON
Modelled on an English parish church, Yangon's cathedral was a focal point for the British community.

MOSQUE, MOULMEIN
The port city of Moulmein, capital of Mon State, was the British administrative centre in the early 19th century.

INDIAN EMBASSY, YANGON

*Embassies in Yangon are housed in some of Asia's finest examples of
19th-century architecture.*

116

HILLSIDE RETREATS, KALAW
During the summer British administrators would often retreat to the cool hills of Kalaw, Shan State, to escape the heat of Yangon.

ENGLISH COUNTRY GARDEN, YANGON

The ex-Vietnamese embassy is one of a number of colonial houses to be found in and around Yangon.

CHAPTER FOUR

PWE~DAW~MYA
Festivals and Festivities

By Khin Myo Chit

119

'The Burman attends all feasts and festivals because it is an unchangeable custom to do so; because everybody else will be there and he enjoys being in a crowd; because he can array himself in his best gaung-baung, and will find all the ladies there similarly arrayed; and, most of all, because whatever the occasion of the festival, it will be a splendid feast.'

H P Cochrane, Amongst the Burmans *(1904)*

A quick meal at a food stall during festivities provides a welcome break.

Festival-goers wait expectantly for the nat-kadaw (spirit wife) to dance.

FESTIVALS ARE A CENTRAL THEME of life in Myanmar. For townsfolk they are an excuse to take a few days off work and visit relations in other parts of the country. For paddy farmers they are a well-earned rest after bringing in the harvest. For craftsmen, such as weavers, basket makers and lacquerware makers, they are a chance to sell their wares; and for actors and musicians they are a constant source of revenue.

Most festivals coincide with the full moons and are Buddhist in origin. Some are major 'gazetted' festivals while others, such as the *nat-pwe* (spirit festivals), though not part of mainstream Buddhism, are nevertheless celebrated with great enthusiasm. Festivals have many common features: the ablution of *nats*, offerings to the monastery, music and dancing, merchants and hawkers, pilgrims, and plenty of food and drink.

Myanmar's new year falls in the second week of April and is ushered in with the water festival, THINGYAN. Although Buddhist in spirit, the festival represents the time when Thagyarmin, king of the celestials, visits the earth for three days. Thagyarmin, a being with a life-span of aeons, was entrusted with the duty of ensuring that the Buddha's teachings flourished on earth. Every new year he reminds people of their spiritual duties.

New year is the time for people to cleanse themselves, make up for omissions in the previous year and to resolve to do better in the coming year. People keep fasts, give alms and do good deeds. The poor fetch water for older folks and wash their hair, and there is goodwill throughout the community – ensuring an auspicious start to the new year.

The true spirit of the water festival has survived in small towns and villages, where people have gentle fun sprinkling scented water on each other in a symbolic act of cleansing. In Yangon and other big cities, however, it has become fashionable to douse everyone with water from huge fire hoses. During *Thingyan* people also sweep the pagoda precincts, wash statues of the Buddha, cook alms for the monks, and collect contributions for ubiquitous novitiation ceremonies.

In KASON, the second month, water is again poured, this time on the sacred *bodhi* tree – the tree of enlightenment. The full moon of *Kason* marks a three-fold anniversary: the birth of Siddhartha, the future Buddha; his attainment of Enlightenment at the foot of the *bodhi* tree; and the eventual passing of the Buddha into *Nirvana*.

On that day, according to folk songs and plays, Siddhartha sat under the *bodhi* tree and the words of the *Anekajatisangsarung*, a song of triumph, poured from his lips. After 45 years of teaching the Truth he became the Buddha and passed away to *Nirvana*. Buddhists celebrate these anniversaries by giving alms, keeping the Buddha's precepts and practising meditation. Everyone goes to the pagoda, accompanied by musicians, singers and dancers, to pour water on the *bodhi* tree.

By NAYONE, the third month, the monsoon has arrived. The sunny days and light showers are chased away by dark storms bringing torrential rain. For adults it is a time to curl up on a sofa with a good book and, for children, a time to gather around to hear stories about the rains.

According to legend the monsoons were the result of warfare among the gods in the skies above. The booming thunder recalls the sound of the celestial drum beaten by Thagyarmin while the lightning flashes represent the clash of arms between Thagyarmin's forces and the Asuras, beings who lived in the celestial abode but had fallen from grace. Raindrops came from the melting clouds above as the two armies fought.

The *Tripitaka* (scripture) examinations for monks and nuns are also held in *Nayone*. Lay people accommodate the candidates and offer daily alms. Apart from written examinations candidates must also recite all the scriptures by rote. The tiny number who pass the recitation tests are showered with honours and gifts.

WASO marks the beginning of Lent, a time for sobriety, self-denial and religious contemplation. At dawn, *neik-ban-saws* (the ushers into heaven) go from house to house announcing the start of the day and reminding people of their duties. Although rarely seen in Yangon these volunteers

In Nayone, the third month, great tropical storms rage over Yangon.

are still active in Mandalay and other towns and villages throughout Myanmar. Dressed in white they carry silver bowls to collect coins, and three-legged lacquer trays with sets of small bowls inside for the food, all of which is donated to monasteries. A huge triangular brass gong is struck to announce their arrival in the neighbourhood.

Marriages are taboo during Lent as are courting and moving home. These are practical, rather than religious, rules as the monsoon season is always a busy time for the farmers. The full moon of *Waso* is also the anniversary of the Buddha's first sermon at Isipatana, a deer park outside Benares in India, 25 centuries ago. It was there that he spoke of the Four Noble Truths: suffering, the origin of suffering, the cessation of suffering and the path that leads to its cessation.

By WAGAUNG the monsoon is in full swing and it is a busy time for the paddy growers. Fields are ploughed and paddy plants are ready to be transplanted by village girls. Young men, who have finished ploughing the fields, serenade them as they work. The music, with its drums and cymbals, is meant to be evocative of the thunder rolling in from over the hills.

Wagaung is also the time for the *Maha Dok* festival whereby alms are given by casting lots. According to custom communities solicit donors to offer alms bowls, and the monks are invited to cast lots for the bowls. Each donor is given a number for his bowl and lots are cast for the

The unusual technique of rowing standing upright takes place on Inle Lake.

winning number. The winner receives a sum of money, which is normally donated to the monastery.

The monsoon is over by TAWTHALIN (September). Sunny days are around the corner and romance is in the air. The wedding ban will be lifted in October and lovers begin to make wedding plans. The community prepares for the annual boat races on rivers and lakes throughout Myanmar: sailing and boat racing were favourite sports of Myanmar's kings, and regattas were always held under royal patronage.

The most spectacular boat race takes place at the Phaung Daw U pagoda on Inle Lake around late September or early October, depending on the full moon. Four or five gilded images of the Buddha are placed on the royal barge and the procession moves from village to village around the lake, stopping at each monastery. On the last day of the festival a boat race takes place with three long-boats, containing 100 people each, rowing with their legs in the traditional Inle style.

THADINGYUT marks the end of Lent and the beginning of festivities. It is the time for the three-day festival of lights to celebrate the anniversary of the Buddha's return from the celestial abode. On the full-moon night of *Thadingyut* the Buddha is said to have descended to earth attended by celestials who created a pathway of stars to light his way. Nowadays streets, houses and public buildings are illuminated and festooned with coloured light-bulbs, while small earthen bowls filled with sesame oil – *see-mee* lights – are placed on the terraces of pagodas in small towns and villages. The story of the Buddha's descent is often acted out on the streets and in pagoda precincts.

It is also a time for remembering people who are owed respect and gratitude. During *Thadingyut* people pay their respects to parents, teachers, relatives and friends, and elderly citizens usually receive small gifts from young people in the community. On bended knee they request forgiveness for any wrong they might have done them in this life or in previous lives.

Another festival of lights – *Tazaungdine* – is held in the month of TAZAUNGMONE (November). Originally held in honour of the guardian gods of the planet, *Tazaungdine* is now treated as a Buddhist festival. It is the time when new robes are given to monks as they prepare for their trips to pay respects to their own teachers, parents and relatives. The community offers gifts to the order (*sangha*) as a whole, rather than to individual monks, an act which earns more merit as the Buddha taught that people should not become partial or attached to individuals.

Robes and other gifts – called *kathina* gifts – are hung on triangular wooden structures (*padetha* trees) in market-places or marquees by the roadside. Everyone contributes a small gift, such as towels, napkins, cups, soap, cakes or *kyat* notes. A procession attended by musicians, dancers and troupes of young girls dressed in their best bright silks then takes the tree laden with gifts to the monastery. *Tazaungdine* also has a weaving festival in which young girls make robes by the light of the full moon, the results of which are donated to the monks.

By NAT-TAW (December) the cold season has arrived. In Yangon the weather is pleasant but in Upper Myanmar and the northern hill areas it is very cold. As the fields fill with ripening grain, communities celebrate with pagoda festivals and ritual feasts in honour of the *nats,* the traditional family gods, celestials and wandering spirits. The feasts are held either by individual families, neighbours or the community.

122

A marquee is set up and images of the *nat* are built, with offerings of flowers, fruit and candles placed before them. An orchestra is hired along with a professional medium – *nat-kadaw* (spirit wife) – who dances as she becomes possessed by the *nat*. The music is rollicking, alcohol flows freely, and everyone in the audience joins in the singing and dancing.

The sunny days and cool, dew-drenched nights of *PYATHO* are perfect for pagoda festivals. Most of Myanmar's festivals are held during this month. Townsfolk and villagers alike erect long, winding rows of stalls around the pagoda, and goods from all over the country go on sale – local glazed earthenware, boxes, baskets, cotton garments and all manner of household goods. In rural areas tradespeople move from place to place in bullock carts or boats to meet up with relations. Not only do they have a good time, they also gain merit by paying respects to elderly relations and making offerings to temples.

In *TABO-DWE*, the eleventh month, the rice-harvesting festival is held. A special sweetmeat made of sticky rice (*kaukhnyin*), ginger, coconut, sesame seeds, peanuts and oil, is prepared to mark the festival, which is celebrated either communally or in a small circle of family and friends. Preparing the sweetmeat is hard work. Girls winnow the

rice grains and shell peanuts, while the boys and men collect and prepare coconuts. Shredded ginger, rice, coconut and peanuts are put into a giant iron pot sizzling with oil; as the mixture becomes thicker, the men stir the concoction. Sesame seeds are added last and the family gathers round to enjoy the delicacy.

The last month of Myanmar's calendar is *TABAUNG* (March) when days are warm and nights are cool and pleasant. *Tabaung* is also a month of festivals as the harvest is safely home and people can look forward to more days of leisure. *Tabaung* is marked by the building of sand stupas, a tradition which comes from the story of a poor labourer who built a sand stupa because he could not afford to build a real one. His good deed was noticed by the Buddha and he embarked on a cycle of glorious lives in which he lacked for nothing.

One of the highlights of the season in Yangon is the Shwedagon pagoda festival that celebrates the enshrinement of eight sacred-hair relics of the Buddha in the pagoda. It is impossible to overlook the festival because the grounds around the Shwedagon are filled with market stalls, merry-go-rounds and ferris wheels. Families visit the pagoda to watch musicians and dancers performing in the precincts, and to buy goods from artisans and craftsmen from all over Myanmar.

Food stalls groan with delicacies such as noodles with thick fish soup, chicken curry with coconut, pancakes, lentil and spice patties, and sweetmeats of sticky rice stuffed with coconut, banana and jaggery. Like all festivals in Myanmar everyone lets their hair down and has a lot of fun. Forgetting their worldly cares, the people of Myanmar live, as Buddhists, for the moment – casting aside all thoughts of how they may feel the next day and heartily entering into the spirit of the celebration.

KHIN MYO CHIT *was born in Yangon in 1915 and was features editor of 'The Guardian Daily'. Her English publications include 'Colourful Burma' and 'Anawrahta of Burma', a historical novel based on the life of the 11th-century King of Bagan.*

A nat statuette stands beside offerings of fruit, incense and flowers.

123

WELCOMING THE BUDDHIST NEW YEAR
*'All over Burma, from the smallest jungle hamlet to the crowded streets
of Yangon and the straggling suburbs of Mandalay, the New Year is
ushered in with…perennial enthusiasm.'*
Sway Yoe, The Burman, His Life and Notions *(1882)*

CELEBRATIONS AFLOAT
*Ceremonial barges celebrate Thingyan pwe, the great water festival,
on the Royal Lake, Yangon.*

TEAM SPIRIT

Long boats in the water festival are rowed by teams using their legs as the fishermen do on Inle Lake.

WATER, WATER EVERYWHERE
'*Before breakfast everyone is soaked, but no one changes...and no one escapes...for the wetting is considered a compliment.*'
Shway Yoe, The Burman, His Life and Notions *(1882)*

THINGYAN, NEW YEAR WATER FESTIVAL

The Buddhist new year is celebrated with water-throwing, and Buddha images and pagodas are washed for New Year's Day. Water symbolises the purification of past wrongs and mistakes. Traditionally a small bowl of scented water was thrown over passers-by to 'cleanse' them. Nowadays revellers use anything they can get their hands on from buckets to fire-hoses.

PHAUNG DAW U FESTIVAL, INLE LAKE

Usually held in late September/early October this is one of the most spectacular festivals in Myanmar. Four of the Buddha images from Phaung Daw U pagoda are rowed around the lake in an imitation royal Karaweik (barge) on a tour of other pagodas around the lake. Boat races are held on the lake during the festival.

ZAT-PWE ARTIST, BAGAN

Myanmar's traditional dancers originally performed Jataka tales before
the royal court. Actors and singers wear the same costumes and use
archaic court language for contemporary performances.

THE DANCER

'In a moment the girl began to dance. But at first it was not a dance, it
was a rhythmic nodding, posturing and twisting of the elbows...like a
jointed doll, and yet incredibly sinuous.'
George Orwell, Burmese Days *(1934)*

MASTERS OF THE STAGE
Marionette theatre was far more popular than live drama from the
early 19th century to the beginning of the 20th.

NAT-KADAWS

'The principal performer at the nat-pwe is the nat-kadaw, which literally means the nat's wife...he is part shaman, part medium, something of an oracle and a healer. Sometimes counsellor, he will offer solace to his neighbours in the village.'

Yves Rodrigue, Nat-Pwe, Burma's Supernatural Sub-Culture *(1992)*

PUPPET MAGIC

*'The puppeteer, however skilled, was actually only the secondary figure
in the troupe. It was only when his art was combined with those of the
musician and puppet-singer that it could work its magic.'*
Ma Thanegi, The Illusion of Life *(1994)*

YOKE-THEI PWE, MARIONETTE THEATRE

*Puppets were introduced into Myanma theatre in the 11th century
to get around the convention that men and women should not dance
closely together in public.*

ON GUARD

Chinthe — mythical lion-like sentinels — guard the approaches to many pagodas and temples.

MR HANDSOME

Nga Tin De statue at the Sarabha Gateway, Bagan. Nga Tin De, also known as Mr Handsome, was a blacksmith who lived in 4th-century Pagan. The king wanted to kill him and take his sister, but the brother and sister escaped and eventually became nats.

MOUNT POPA, HOME OF THE MAHAGIRI NATS

*During Nayon (May to June) pilgrims flock to Mount Popa to
celebrate the annual Festival of the Spirits. Mount Popa (Sanskrit for
flower) is about 80 km south-east of Bagan and stands 1,519 m
high. From the 4th to the 11th centuries every king had to make a
pilgrimage there to consult the spirits before his reign could begin.*

MAKING LACQUERWARE, BAGAN

Bagan is famous for its lacquerware. Originally from China, Myanmar's earliest-known surviving piece of lacquerware dates from 1274.

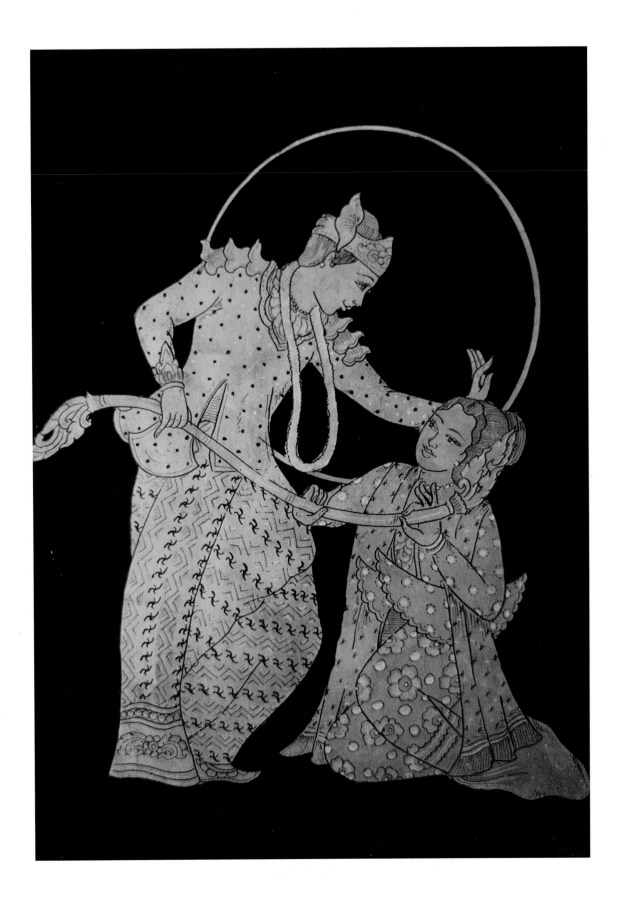

ZAT DRAMA

*Myanmar's classical Zat dramas are based on Indian Jataka tales, also
known as the Ramayana.*

CHAPTER FIVE

HKALAY THU~ NGEH~MYA

Children of Myanmar

By Dr Kyi Kyi Tin-Myint

141

'The sheer joy of life abides in them, and they seem to live perpetually at play; in the village street where they play a game of ninepins with the great seeds of a jungle creeper; in the monastery where they lie upon the floor and scream out their lessons with lusty delight; in the river where they splash and plunge before they can walk...and at the pagoda where they hold flowers before them with faces screwed up to gravity, with laughter pent up behind it.'

V C Scott O'Connor, The Silken East *(1904)*

Schoolchildren wait for the next bus home after school is over for the day.

MANY YEARS AGO WHEN I WAS a young medical student at the Yangon Institute of Medicine I took part in a field trip to the foothills of the Bago Yoma mountains. We visited a small village cut off from the developing towns and cities of the delta. The community was very traditional – the men worked as farmers or fishermen and the women as seamstresses or potters. It had a few houses, a small whitewashed pagoda and a monastery where the youngest children were taught by the monks to read and write. The older children went to school in a nearby town, crossing a bridge over a small valley through which a stream flowed in the monsoon season.

My colleagues and I set up a one-day medical clinic which was a great success as many of the villagers were either too ill or too poor to travel to the nearby town for treatment. The villagers showed their gratitude by inviting us to their houses for celebratory meals. In all there were 70 families and we knew that each one would be heartbroken if we refused their hospitality. Yet it was impossible to visit them individually. In the end we decided it would be most diplomatic if we visited some for lunch, others for tea and the rest for dinner. Of course we could accept only a taste of the many delicious dishes on offer.

At the end of the day, groaning with too much food, we returned to our minibus only to find that it had been loaded up with all kinds of delicacies, a parting gift from the villagers. There were enormous bags of rice, large tins of sesame oil, baskets brimming with groundnuts and lentils, bundles of salted fish, dried shrimp, smoked lobster, preserved venison and mounds of fruits and vegetables. We were astounded by their generosity.

As we thanked the villagers I caught sight of a small group of young children sitting on the ground in the cool shade of a huge banyan tree. Like all children in Myanmar their faces broke into great wide grins as I approached them. They were pointing at something on the ground: it was a small tortoise with a brown and black shell. A boy of five or six with sparkling brown eyes held it up to me. 'Oh, be careful,' I said. 'Don't drop it, it might break.'

A young novice monk washes an alms bowl after the morning meal.

142

'Oh no,' they laughed. 'We won't hurt it. We were just wondering how fast it can run.'

Smiling and joking, the children accompanied me back to the minibus and, as I walked, I was vaguely aware of someone tugging at my shoulder bag. I put my hand inside my bag for a notebook and felt a strange, smooth surface. They had slipped the tortoise into my bag; another leaving present! I lifted it out carefully and gave it back to one of the children. 'It really is very kind of you,' I said, 'but what am I going to do with a tortoise for rest of my life?' They all laughed and offered me the poor creature once again. 'But you liked the tortoise so much we wanted you to have it!' they all cried.

The gentle faces of those laughing village children remained with me for a long time. I recalled them very vividly one day more than 20 years later when I arrived with my husband and children in the US, where I had gone to take up an intern's post at Cook County Hospital, Chicago. In the airport lobby I heard a piercing cry and noticed a young woman desperately trying to control her two small children. Aggressive, surly and demanding they argued noisily with their parents and threw a tantrum unaware of the embarrassment they were causing. I was shocked: up till that point I had considered myself to be rather cosmopolitan and, well, westernised, but the sight of those spoilt and angry children vividly highlighted the clear cultural divide between my old and my new country.

In Myanmar it is rare to see children crying, squabbling or being rude to their parents. I myself only argued with my mother on one occasion. I was 17 and she had caught me talking alone with a boy. My mother had told me off saying it was not 'proper' for a young woman to behave in this way, while I had argued back that she was being unfair. The sense of shame I felt then, when I saw how much I had upset her, has remained with me for more than 40 years.

Although a long time has passed since my own childhood in Myanmar, and many things have changed, children still have a special place in society. Children are welcomed as blessings – indeed they are known as 'gem sons' or 'gem daughters' who give joy, act as vehicles for the fulfilment of parental duties and offer affectionate support in old age. A little boy is often called *tha shwe yay* ('wrought in gold' or 'as precious as gold') and he is loved for his beauty rather than for being good. Girls, on the other hand, are expected to be quiet and thoughtful; *thamie laimma* ('she listens to her mother and father') is the highest compliment a young girl can ever receive.

Children are socialised at a very early age by working, playing and helping adults. No special activity is devised for children although most have simple toys and play together. They usually join in with whatever the adults happen to be doing, whether it is carrying a baby brother, peeling and cutting vegetables or picking fruit. Extended family relatives and neighbours are allowed to play a part in looking after and disciplining the children, a factor which reinforces the child's sense of community.

By the time a child is 12 he or she is entrusted to carry out a number of duties for the family – to cook simple meals, pick fruit, wash clothes, mind a baby, prepare *thanaka* (bark paste) cream and make simple sales and purchases at the market. Up to that age boys and girls play happily together and have much the same duties and responsibilities within the family group.

143

Thanaka (bark paste) protects the skin of a young woman and her baby.

After the age of 12 the paths of boys and girls begin to diverge. Puberty was traditionally marked by the ear-piercing ceremony for girls and the *Shinbyu* (novitiation) ceremony for boys, although families are much more flexible about their timing these days. A *Shinbyu* is a huge family event as it gives parents the opportunity to accrue great merit (*kusala*) in the community, and in future lives, while it reaffirms the boy's great *kan* (good fortune) in being born male – the form in which the Buddha attained *Nirvana*.

As teenagers girls are encouraged to take more responsibility in the home and develop a feminine manner. They are taught to be well-groomed, to walk and sit in a feminine way and, if they leave the house, they must be accompanied, even if it is only by their younger brothers and sisters.

Socially girls mix with female friends and relations, visiting pagodas, shops, stage shows and cinemas. The girl takes on extra tasks at home such as sewing, helping the mother with her younger siblings, advanced cookery, carrying flowers to the shrine and preparing alms for the monks. She must also learn the family business, if there is one, and will only continue her studies if the family can spare her, although many more families are now realising the importance of a full education for girls.

144

A family at prayer. The flowers they hold are offerings for the shrines.

Boys, on the other hand, find that their schooling becomes more important than household duties once they reach their teens. Most boys attend secondary schools until 16 and many go on to further study. Schools are based on the British system introduced in the colonial era. Before that they would attend monasteries for their education, where they would learn Buddhist scriptures, arithmetic, poetry and perhaps elementary astronomy and medicine.

Buddhism is very much at the heart of Myanma society. Like most religions it is family oriented and actually places parents and teachers in the same lofty hierarchy as Buddha, his scriptures and the *sangha* (order of monks). Families visit the temple together, where they are reminded of their duty to observe and practise the five fundamental concepts of self-discipline: not to kill, lie, commit adultery, steal or take intoxicants. From a very early age, therefore, the child learns the importance of these basic rules for living.

Buddhism also teaches the child to be gentle and passive, rather than aggressive and demanding. In Myanmar small children rarely scream, fight or argue with siblings and friends. Perhaps this is because they receive a lot of attention from parents, extended family members and neighbours.

In this close-knit and caring environment children grow up with a sense of trust in the world. They are not discouraged from talking to strangers because no one could imagine anyone ever hurting or taking advantage of a child. Even strangers address each other as 'auntie', 'uncle', 'sister', 'brother', 'grandpa' and 'grandma', and it is rude to call people by their name unless they are younger than oneself. Social problems such as emotional deprivation, physical and sexual abuse or child prostitution, which are prevalent in the West and parts of south-east Asia, are practically unheard of in Myanmar.

While they are growing up, then, children can expect a loving, predictable and trustworthy world where their lives are structured and their responsibilities clearly defined. In return they must show self-discipline and respect for their elders. Buddhism reinforces this message, imbuing children with a strong sense of duty to repay their parents for the sacrifice they have made. This rests lightly on most children, who gladly look after their parents and relations in old age. There is no need for nursing homes in Myanmar as parents and extended family members live with their children. Frankly they are a good investment.

This close and loving environment in their early years explains why most people are extraordinarily friendly and generous. In Myanmar it is not a problem, but there are drawbacks when travelling abroad.

I experienced some myself when I arrived in the United States in 1971. I was 40 years old and a mother of six children yet, by American standards, extremely naive and innocent. Buddhism had taught me to be quiet, gentle and self-effacing, yet everyone around me was aggressive and extremely vociferous. Colleagues at the hospital said I would never survive at Cook County, which had 3,500 beds and was located in the poorest part of Chicago. I did and subsequently went on to take up a new post in New York's infamous Harlem Hospital, where there were regular shoot-outs in the hospital lobby. Strangely enough I was never afraid. The uncomplicated view of the world I had acquired during my upbringing in Myanmar had, in a roundabout way, prepared me for even the worst extremes of society.

This outlook on life reminds me of the incident in 1948, on the eve of Myanmar's independence, when Britain's great wartime leader, Sir Winston Churchill, controversially remarked that Myanma people were too childlike to survive as an independent nation. In Myanmar we were outraged. But, looking back, I think perhaps we did not see the real meaning behind his words. I believe now that he was simply remarking on the rare qualities of the people of Myanmar – trust, honesty, gentleness, generosity, piety and respect – qualities which Myanma people learn in childhood and, unlike most peoples, never forget.

DR KYI KYI TIN-MYINT is a practising child psychiatrist and author of 'Koko Maung and Myananda' (1993), a novel, and 'The Collected Poems and Short Stories of Kyi Aye' (1993) written under her pen name.

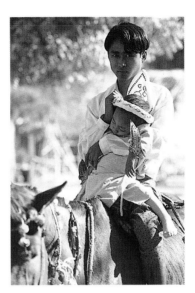

A sleepy Shinbyu prince is escorted to the monastery on horseback.

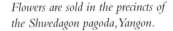

Flowers are sold in the precincts of the Shwedagon pagoda, Yangon.

145

WATCHING MOTHER
Women throughout Myanmar smoke enormous hand-rolled cheroots
and it is not uncommon to see small children doing the same.

SUNDAY BEST
'Children's clothes are unknown...in Burma, and every little girl is
dressed like her mother, from her sandals to the flowers in her hair.'
V C Scott O'Connor, The Silken East *(1904)*

FROM BOY TO PRINCE
Carefree youngsters play outside the Ananda temple, Bagan. Every
Buddhist boy is expected to become a monk for a short time. For this
he must take part in a Shinbyu ceremony which involves being dressed
in elaborate clothes as a prince.

A CHILD'S PRAYER
Lost in worship a small girl kneels before a monk in the precinct of the
Shwedagon pagoda, Yangon.

MAKING A SPLASH

Most youngsters love water whether it is swimming practice for Yangon schoolchildren or a welcome shower for a village toddler.

152

BUDDHIST NUN
Although some young girls enter nunneries, few then choose to follow
a religious life.

FAMILY VALUES

From the age of seven or eight young girls are expected to help their
mothers look after younger siblings.

BUFFALO PLAYGROUND (PREVIOUS PAGE)
'…they [children] grow up merry, naked little things, sprawling in the
dust of the gardens, sleeping in the sun with their arms round the
village animals.'
H Fielding, The Soul of a People *(1899)*

DIVIDED YOUTH
*Boys and girls grow up together as babies but they are separated in
their school days. Most Buddhists begin their schooling at the local
monastery but some girls, especially in rural communities, are sent out
to work when they are young and have little chance of an education.*

158

HERDING THE FLOCK

Children, such as this young boy from Bagan, help their families by looking after the domestic animals.

159

PAST, PRESENT AND FUTURE

*Today's children — Myanmar's future — lost in thought among the
ruins of Bagan, part of their glorious heritage.*

YOUNG SCHOLARS
*'Every Buddhist boy in the country is taught to read and write and
in this respect, at least, there are but very few illiterate Burmans.'*
Shway Yoe, The Burman, His Life and Notions *(1882)*

SMILING EYES
*'In them [the children] the liveliness and happiness of the Burmese
race is crossed with no flaw.'*
V C Scott O'Connor, The Silken East *(1904)*

CHAPTER SIX

HSIN LOK~THA

Working Elephants

By Richard Gayer

163

'Some of the timber elephants like tea. There was the case of Ma Chew (Miss Pretty), who with her mother would punctually turn up before my tent at about 4 o'clock, grabbing with relish and shamelessly whatever was on the camp-table – bread, biscuits, cakes, sugar and fruit. One day, having inadvertently wrapped her trunk around a hot cup of tea, Ma Chew screamed in shock, turned her back on me, as cross as two sticks, and for quite a time declined with dignity any liquid offered to her in a tea cup.'

U Tok Gale, Burmese Timber Elephant *(1974)*

A young tusker picks his way through undergrowth and fallen logs.

The elephants and their oozies (riders) set out for the forest.

HIGH IN THE REMOTE AND MOUNTAINOUS country where the best teak grows, a mature teak tree is skilfully felled by two men using axes and a cross saw. The great tree plunges hundreds of metres down into a ravine, tearing a swathe through thick undergrowth and landing with a crash in a cloud of dust and leaves.

After the tree has been sawn into logs powerful bull elephants are sent down into the ravine to haul the logs back up to the dragging trail. Two immense tuskers, one pulling with a harness and dragging chains and the other pushing with its head and tusks from behind, begin to shift a three-tonne log up the steep slope. '*Yu ko gyi! yu!*' yells the rider of the lead elephant, '*Pull big brother! Pull!*'. Snorting and bellowing, the elephant strains forward and the log begins to move upwards. '*Aung! Aung!*' shouts the rider of the second elephant, '*Push! Push!*'. His animal gets down on its knees and with tremendous force pushes the log forwards with the base of its trunk, its tusks ploughing deep furrows in the black earth.

These animals and their *oozies* (riders) are part of an army of elephants and men who each year extract more than a million tonnes of teak and other hardwoods from Myanmar's deciduous monsoon forests. Because of the great value of teak, elephant-logging has developed over many years into a fine art requiring the ultimate elephant-riding skills and the most highly-trained elephants. For two centuries or more the story of Myanmar's elephants and the story of teak have been inextricably intertwined.

During the logging season timber elephants drag, push, lift and roll hundreds of thousands of logs – some weighing as much as five tonnes – through dense forest, precipitous mountain terrain, up and down impossibly steep gullies and gorges, sometimes launching them over cliffs and precipices. Powerful tuskers manipulate logs with head, tusks, trunk and feet, their skill and intelligence as important as that of their riders in carrying out this difficult and dangerous work.

During the monsoon months teams of elephants and riders work together in swirling water and deep mud, launching the teak logs into the streams and rivers in which they are floated out of the forests to towns and cities throughout the country.

This apparently antiquated system of forestry, known as the Burma Selection System, is in fact the world's only large-scale system of sustainable natural tropical forestry, in terms of both sustained-yield logging and conservation of forest ecosystems. It was devised by the great 19th-century botanist Dietrich Brandis, an early environmentalist and conservationist. He set standards of forest management which have probably never been equalled, blending German scientific forestry with centuries-old Myanma methods.

In the Brandis system teak trees are selected, felled and extracted on a 30-year cycle. This allows natural regeneration of teak from the growing stock of smaller trees and disturbs the ecosystem as little as possible. Elephants extract the carefully-selected timber through dense forest and steep hillsides with an almost surgical precision, leaving the surrounding forest intact and inaccessible. Extraction by elephants causes so little forest disturbance that within a few months barely a trace remains of the little damage done.

Elephant-extracted timber is Myanmar's biggest export, generating several hundred million US dollars per annum, accounting for more than 40 per cent of gross overseas earnings. In spite of high levels of deforestation, Myanmar still has more forest left than any other country in continental Asia, including 70 per cent of the world's natural teak. The managers, foresters and elephant vets of the Myanma Timber Enterprise and the Forest Department have successfully maintained Myanmar's forestry system since independence. But the forests, like tropical forests everywhere, are under threat from population pressure and increasing demand for timber. The rapid introduction of industrialised and mechanised forestry could undermine the environmentally-sound principles of the Brandis system and threaten the long-term survival of Myanmar's forests, elephants and elephant-riding communities.

With almost two-thirds of the world's working elephants, Myanmar is the last country in Asia with a thriving elephant culture, and the only country where the

An oozie gives instructions to his elephant with subtle knee movements.

elephant is of overwhelming economic importance. Whole communities depend entirely on the skills of capturing, taming and training elephants and working with them. The elephant riders come from several of the country's ethnic groups, including the lowland Burmese, Shans, Tai Hkampti and Yaw as well as the Karen, Kachin and Kadu hill tribes.

Many elephant riders are born into families who have worked with elephants for generations, the skills passed down from father to son. An elephant rider may work with one elephant for decades – the longest and one of the closest relationships that man has with any animal.

> 'A baby boy may be born in an elephant camp and at the same moment an elephant calf may be being born a mile or two away in the jungle. That child and that elephant may grow up together, play together, work together all their working lives and may still be familiar friends when sixty years have passed.'
> J H Williams, Elephant Bill *(1950)*

Rider and elephant thus learn to understand each other perfectly and become almost part of one another. The older men have a profound knowledge of the elephant, both wild and domesticated. A good rider must always be firm, kind and even-tempered controlling the elephant entirely by word of command, by signals delivered with toe and knee and by movements of his body. He should not have to use a loud or harsh voice. These skills can only be acquired over many years. It is astonishing to see what a skilled man can make his elephant do, his orders given in such a quiet way that the elephant's movements often appear spontaneous.

A good rider must also be skilled at approaching, catching, fettering and subduing unruly or dangerous animals, and he is responsible for every aspect of his elephant's health and well-being. He must save it from unnecessary exertion and exposure, ensure it is adequately fed and watered, wash and examine every part of its body daily and be able to treat it for common ailments.

In spite of this close relationship the elephants are not pets. Powerful bull elephants can be very dangerous, capable of killing a man in an instant. Their riders must constantly be alert for subtle changes in behaviour that indicate the onset of *musth,* a period associated with sexual activity and social hierarchy in bull elephants, when they become more aggressive towards each other and towards humans. Yet *oozies* take great pride in their skills, and many men will willingly ride an elephant that is known to be dangerous.

Timber elephants are unquestionably the most intelligent and highly-trained of all domestic animals, yet, paradoxically, they are also the least domesticated. After the day's work they are released into the forest where they can socialise with their own kind and feed on bamboo and grasses. Timber elephants are physically and psychologically healthier than captive elephants and will breed readily, unlike those in captivity.

At the start of the logging season, soon after the arrival of the monsoon in May or June, the elephant men move from their villages to the logging camps deep in the reserved teak forests. The camps are clustered in forest tracts chosen each year for selective extraction. Life in the camps is extremely hard and often dangerous. Some are three to four days' walk from the nearest river or track. At the height of the rains some camps become completely isolated as streams and rivers turn into raging torrents and become impassable.

Work begins before dawn with a search for elephants that have wandered off during the night. Teams of elephants

166

An oozie and his elephant may grow up together and work as a team for decades.

are assigned to different duties – stumping, dragging, transport, lining up logs in the floating streams, stacking logs at loading points, launching teak, breaking and dismantling log jams and stream-clearing. Timber elephants have an astonishing ability to work steep mountainsides, moving safely over precipitous and slippery trails that would defeat mules, horses or any machine. When descending a slope too steep for ordinary walking an elephant may sit down on its vast backside and slide. Or it may lie down on its belly with its hind legs trailing out behind and crawl head first.

> *'Dragging a log weighing four tons while negotiating a high, narrow ledge is risky business. But an elephant can judge what is safe to the nearest inch, working with endless patience. Both rider and elephant know that should the log start to slide or roll over the ledge all the gear and harness can be got rid of in the twinkling of an eye. The elephant has only to whip round in his tracks, step inside the chain, and bend down his head for all the harness to peel off as easily as a girl will lift a slip over her shoulders.'*
>
> *Ibid*

Throughout its working life an elephant never stops learning. It does not work mechanically like other animals, but uses its intelligence to solve the endless problems that arise in the dangerous work of shifting huge logs over difficult terrain, through thick mud or in fast-flowing water. But the elephant's intelligence and ingenuity can also be used for deception:

> *'Many young elephants develop the naughty habit of plugging up the wooden bell, or kalouk, that they wear around their necks with mud or clay so that the clappers cannot ring, in order to steal silently into a grove of cultivated bananas at night, eating not only the bananas and the leaves but the entire tree as well, just beside the hut of the owner of the grove and without waking him or his family.'*

> *Ibid*

During the torrential rains of the early monsoon the elephants have to launch the previous season's harvest of teak into streams, and must keep the timber moving by relaunching logs stranded at bends, on sand bars or against underwater obstacles – an operation known as *ye laik*. They must work at any time, often at night by the light of bamboo torches. Highly-trained elephants, sometimes swimming without riders, may be used to break log-jams: often the elephant itself will remove the key log in order to release the jam.

The forests are hot, wet and humid during the rainy season but later, from September to January, the first part of the dry season, they are cool, green and shady. This is the time when the the capture, taming and training of young elephants takes place. Every year the Forest Department determines the number of elephants that can be captured under the Elephant Control Scheme; elephant capture is a dangerous and delicate operation requiring the best *oozies* and highly-trained elephants called *kunkees*. Nowadays the traditional lassoo method, *kyaw hpan,* has been replaced by immobilisation with tranquillising darts.

Taming a young elephant – whether wild or captive-bred – involves immobilising it in a *crush* (an enclosed wooden pen), and weakening its spirit by depriving it of sleep and food. At the same time it is charmed by hypnotic singing and given morsels of tasty food such as tamarind or salt. After a week or two the calf is slowly taught to accept a rider, but it will be at least 20 years before the elephant is considered fully trained.

Wives and children of elephant riders working in the more remote areas live with them in the forest during the logging season. In March, at the start of the hot, dry season, logging stops, and the forest camps are abandoned. Possessions and young children are loaded onto the backs of the elephants for the long journey back to the summer rest camps.

Now the forests are parched and leafless, and ground fires often sweep through them, burning up the leaf litter. These fires may be started deliberately in order to assist the regeneration of teak, which is fire resistant. But soon after the first monsoon rainstorms, the teak comes into leaf again and the trees flower, producing a mass of white blossom, and the harvesting cycle begins again.

RICHARD GAYER *is an award-winning independent film producer and director. For his current project, a documentary film on timber elephants, he has studied working elephants of Myanmar, Sri Lanka and Thailand, and the tropical forestry in Brazil.*

167

A young elephant manages to drag an enormous log into the forest clearing.

YU KO GYI! (PULL!)

Bellowing under the strain, a young tusker in harness and chains
drags an enormous log out of a forest clearing.

AUNG AUNG! (PUSH!)

*Another tusker concentrates hard as he carefully rolls a huge log down
the steep hillside.*

FIRST SPLASH
A female elephant carefully watches over her new-born calf as he explores the river excitedly.

JOURNEY BACK TO CAMP
Five workers and their riders – oozies – return to the village after a hard day's work. Elephants are strong swimmers and will happily cross even a fast-flowing river.

BATH TIME
At the end of the day, the elephants bathe. They await the oozies who must scrub down the elephants in the river and massage their necks to ensure they are ready for work the next day.

MIGHTY TASK

During the logging season, Myanma timber elephants drag, push, lift and roll hundreds of thousands of logs, some weighing up to five tonnes each.

SPECIAL RELATIONSHIP

'These men [oozies] are born with a knowledge of elephants...They can sit on an elephant from the age of six, and they grow up learning all the traditional knowledge, the myth and the legend...which is attached to this lovable animal.'
Lt-Col J H Williams, Elephant Bill *(1950)*

174

REUNION

Family members greet each other with the friendly gesture of a curling trunk. The oozies, who work with the elephants for a lifetime, become part of the family.

OFF TO WORK

A mighty tusker leads the workers – both men and elephants – into the jungle where they will spend long hours harvesting teak.

CHAPTER SEVEN

TAUNG~BAW~ THA~MYA

People of the Hills

By Mi Mi Khaing[†]

177

'Among the Shans, who were in the majority, wandered in their distinctive costumes members of many tribes…There were Tais, Laos, Kaws, Palaungs, Was and heaven knows what else. The Kaws [Akhas] stand out from among the others by reason of their fine physique and swarthy colour…The women wear a headdress covered with silver beads so that it looks like a helmet; their hair is parted in the middle and comes down over the ears as one sees it in the portraits of the Empress Eugénie, and in middle age they have funny little wrinkled faces full of humour.'

W Somerset Maugham, The Gentleman in the Parlour *(1930)*

From Putao in the north, amazing views of the Himalayas are visible.

This elderly Padaung tribeswoman wears a striking collection of neck rings.

MYANMAR'S FLAG SYMBOLISES THE ethnic diversities of the union in a very graphic way: the red background is said to represent courage, while the white star surrounded by five smaller stars in the top left-hand corner is meant to symbolise the country and its five major ethnic groups – the Shan, the Karen, the Kachin, the Chin and the Burmans (including the Mon and Arakanese who have assimilated with the Burmans).

The Union of Myanmar actually comprises 135 ethnic groups, the largest of which is the Burmans who make up 70 per cent of the population. The Burmans live in the central valley and delta regions of the Ayeyarwaddy River and Arakan and Tenasserim States. Most of the remaining groups occupy Shan State, the massive northern hill region that borders on China, Thailand, Cambodia and India.

The hill tribes are ancestors of peoples who migrated into Myanmar centuries ago. The first migration was by the Mon-Khmer, who entered from Laos and Cambodia and are now represented by small groups of Wa, Tai, Palaung, Yao, Padaung, En and Mon. Tibeto-Burmans then descended from the north and occupied the upper reaches of the Ayeyarwaddy River, going on to establish the Kingdom of Bagan and the later capitals of Toungoo, Ava, Amarapura, Sagaing and Mandalay.

The Kadu, Lashi, Atsi and Arakanese are all descended from the Tibeto-Burmans, as are the Chin-Kachins, Sing-po, Lisu, Lahu, Kaw (Akha) and Ako. Finally, in the 13th century, the Tai-Chinese (Shan) migrated from Yunnan province in southern China.

The Shan sacked Bagan in 1287 and went on to control Upper Myanmar during the 12th and 15th centuries. Although they never managed to overcome internal rivalries for long enough to form an empire, the Shan have nevertheless managed to retain their influence in the region. The Shan territory consisted of 33 sub-states ruled by *sabwas* (feudal lords) assisted by village headmen, who controlled civil, criminal and fiscal matters. Each state, however small, had its own ministers, police force, education system, medical services and public works and had control over its own budget. The British introduced a dual system whereby the *sabwa* ruled alongside colonial officers and founded several important administrative centres – the hill stations of Taunggyi, Loilem, Kalaw, Loimwe, Lashio and Kutkai.

In 1959 the *sabwas* signed over their hereditary rights to the Myanma Government and the area was renamed Shan State. The heart is the Shan Plateau, 1,000 metres above sea level to the west of the River Salween. To the north, east and west of the plateau are mountain ranges running in a north-south direction; to the east, a mass of mountains; to the north, broad valleys and steep slopes rising up to 2,300 metres; and to the west, mountains rolling down to areas of broad plains.

Four million people belonging to 33 different hill tribes live in Shan State. Each tribe occupies a distinct region: the Palaungs in the ranges in the north-west, the Kachins in the far north, the Kaws (Akhas) in the extreme north-east, the Was in the ranges of the north-east and the Padaungs in a corner of the south-west. The Kachins live in Kachin State and Northern Shan State, the Karens mainly in Karen State, the Chin in the Chin Hills and the Mons in the south-east. The Shans themselves occupy the valleys of the Shan Plateau.

Hill tribes have, for the most part, retained their customary dress, language, religions, artistic heritage and culture. Most practise shifting cultivation (the Shans are the exception) – burning a small area of forest, planting rice, corn and other crops for a few years and, when the soil is exhausted, abandoning the land until vegetation replenishes it. Some groups shift fields in a 10-15 year rotation, while others move entire villages. To obtain salt, metal implements and other goods not found in the hills the tribes trade forest products at markets in the valleys.

The best places for visitors to see hill tribes are at the regional Shan markets, which rotate over a five-day period. This begins in Heho, moves to Taunggyi, thence west to Kalaw, a former hill station, finally to Pindaya north-east of Inle Lake.

Naga woman, Khanti, wears the full ceremonial dress of the tribe.

The SHAN were among the first immigrants to the region having migrated from Nanchao in Yunnan province, south-west China, in the 13th century. They won supremacy in the region through control of its rice fields. Although Shan State takes its name from them its population is only 50 per cent ethnic Shan. They are the largest ethnic group in Myanmar comprising around seven per cent of the entire population. They are predominantly Buddhist but unlike other ethnic groups are mainly traders, cultivating rice and vegetables in the valleys for sale rather than for subsistence.

The Shan have a paler complexion than other tribes in the state and are renowned for their cultural and artistic heritage, particularly their silverware, lacquerware, paper and woven bags. Their traditional dress, worn at feasts or formal celebrations, comprises a Chinese-style jacket with a pink, blue or yellow turban. Women wear turbans embroidered with gold or bright primary colours plus a striped *longyi* and tight-fitting jacket. Men often wear baggy black trousers, a cropped jacket and *dah*, a traditional silver sword with a sheath decorated in red and green wool. The *dah* features in the Shan sword dance in which a lithe, tattooed tribesman dances to the accompaniment of drums while two, three or even four *dahs* are brandished around him.

After the Shan the KAREN are the most populous ethnic group constituting six per cent of the population. They live mainly along the Thai border and have 11 sub-groups, including the Kayah (Red Karen), Karenni (Black

179

Karen), Paku (White Karen), Padaung and Taunythu. Most live in mountain villages and practise shifting cultivation. Their houses have thatched roofs and are built on bamboo stilts; domestic animals are kept under the house at night for their protection.

The priest is the most revered person in a Karen village. A ritual leader, he sets dates for annual ceremonies and on his death the Karen relocate the village. Most Karens combine Buddhism with animist beliefs, although American missionaries managed to convert a good proportion of the population (around 20 per cent) at the turn of the century. Luckily for the evangelists a central Karen myth told of a younger 'white brother' who would come across the water bringing writing from God.

Karen are prolific weavers. Men, women and children wear a simple tunic with elaborate stitching. For unmarried girls the tunic is made of white cotton, while mature women wear it as a blouse over a red, white, yellow or black embroidered *longyi*. All Karen wear distinctive cup-shaped earrings decorated with tufts of coloured wool.

The most interesting sub-group of the Karen is the PADAUNG, who live in Loikaw, Kayah State. The men are

farmers growing irrigated crops such as maize, millet and cotton, and raising pigs and cattle. Padaung men are not easily distinguishable from the Shan, unlike their womenfolk, who are quite extraordinary. Dubbed the 'giraffe women' or 'long-necked Karen' Padaung women traditionally wear a stack of brass rings around their necks. Every year, starting in their teens, a woman traditionally adds new rings to her collection until she marries, by which time her neck will have stretched and her shoulders been pushed down, shrinking her head.

The custom of wearing neck rings originated because Padaung men wanted to make their women look unattractive and thereby deter neighbouring tribes from seizing them. They do not appear to have achieved their aim as Padaung women, with their strange uplifted faces, still manage to look oddly attractive.

Myanmar's 30,000 WA are also related to the Karen. Dark-skinned and stocky they live along the borders with China and, until recently, practised headhunting as part of their fertility rites. In popular mythology they were also cannibals and it is said that their old people had to climb trees to escape young tribesmen who wanted to put them in the pot. As always there is some truth in the legend: in Wa society heads (usually from animals) were needed both for fertility rites and blessings for important occasions such as marriages, deaths or the founding of a new village.

Up in the western region of Taunpeng live the PALAUNG, one of the Mon-Khmer tribal peoples related to the Wa. They live in small long-houses on stilts with several families sharing a house. Famous for growing tea there are around 60,000 Palaung in Myanmar.

Palaung traditional dress is perhaps the most colourful and distinctive of all the hill tribes: all women wear white, green, pink, red and blue jackets with a red-striped *longyi*. Married women wear cane rings around their waists and strings of beads around their necks, small red-velvet hats decorated with shells and a long patchwork hood of blue, scarlet and black velvet bordered with white. Older women shave their heads and wear white hoods.

Stilts keep the houses dry during floods in a Naga village on the Chindwin River.

Further south, along the border with Thailand, live the AKHA (Kaw), a Tibeto-Burmese people related to the Chin. They have dark complexions, pronounced noses and round eyes, and the men wear pigtails. Like the Karen the Akha are shifting cultivators growing rice and vegetables on mountainsides. Rice is very important to Akha society and there are many myths and rituals bound up with its cultivation. They believe that the rice plant is a sentient being and that the clearance of rice fields, the planting of the seed, care of the plants and the harvest must all be done according to 'Akha Way', a set of customs which the Akha observe in place of a religion. The Way also demands that people learn the names of 60 male ancestors and keep ancestral altars in their homes where offerings can be made at new year and after the rice harvest.

Akha settlements are distinguished by their high-roofed houses on posts, a village swing which is used in festivals, and sacred gates at the upper and lower ends of the village. Visitors who want to enter an Akha house must first walk through the gates to rid themselves of the jungle spirit.

Women wear short, knee-length kilts and jackets of black cloth decorated with shells, seeds, beads, coins and tassels, together with black leggings and a sash. Their elaborate headdress adorned with heavy silver baubles, coins and jewellery is a masterpiece of Akha craftsmanship. Unmarried girls wear a simple cap, and tie small gourds to their clothes. Akha men usually wear loose Chinese-style black trousers and black embroidered jackets.

The CHIN, who occupy the western mountains, are related to the Naga to the north. Both groups lead a more settled, agricultural life than the Kachins and many are still animist although, like the Wa, some Chin and Nagas practised headhunting. The KACHIN, who comprise between two and three per cent of Myanmar's population, practise slash-and-burn agriculture and are skilled hunters. Their original name was Jinghpaw (Singhpo), which is derived from the Tibetan words *sin-po* meaning cannibal.

The LISU, who live on the borders with Thailand, are also a Tibeto-Burmese people. They grow rice and

The full tribal headdress of this Akha woman is intricately crafted.

vegetables for subsistence high in the mountains, and live in bamboo and wood houses. All Lisu houses have a fireplace and ancestral altar, a bedroom, a large living area and a guest area. Every Lisu village has a shrine for its guardian spirit located above the village in a roofed shrine that women cannot enter. The Lisu also worship Wu Sa, the earth's creator, together with spirits of their ancestors, the forest, the sun and moon.

Lisu men wear simple black jackets, blue or green trousers and black leggings; the women wear long tunics with red sleeves and patterned yokes, black knee-length trousers and red leggings. A wide, black sash is wound around the waist which is then looped with tassels of tightly-woven coloured threads and pom-poms. On special occasions, such as the new year festival, Lisu women wear turbans with coloured tassels, silver jewellery and tunics decorated with silver buttons.

Myanmar's hill tribes, like other tribal peoples throughout the world, are in danger of disappearing as modern society encroaches on their way of life. It is up to us to ensure that the wealth of ancient wisdom, culture and crafts their society holds is preserved for future generations as well as our own.

[†]MI MI KHAING *(1916–90) was an author and social scientist. This essay is based on a series of articles she wrote on Shan State for 'The Nation' newspaper.*

AKHA VILLAGE

Houses are simply constructed from wooden poles, woven matting and strips of bamboo. Visitors to the village must walk through sacred gates in order to rid themselves of the spirit of the jungle.

GATHERING WOOD

Akha girls return from the jungle with baskets of wood. Myanmar's 200,000 Akhas live in the northern border region with Thailand.

THE NEXT GENERATION

A young tribesman. The Akha, who have their origins in Yunnan,
southern China, are shifting cultivators, primarily growing rice and
vegetables on steep mountainsides.

CLEVER FOOTWORK

Molten silver is poured into a cast set in buffalo horn to make the
distinctive silver baubles that adorn the headdresses.

CROWNING GLORY

Akha woman wearing the traditional headdress made up of silver beads, coins and buttons. The elaborate Akha headwear contrasts sharply with their simple plain-weave garments.

187

TRIBAL PARAPHERNALIA
A collector stands alongside his display of traditional Chin musical instruments, spears, vessels for rice liquor, and skulls.

POLE POSITION
A bamboo and rattan hut in a Naga village on the River Chindwin, near Khanti. The houses are built on stilts to avoid hazards such as snakes and floods.

CEREMONIAL DRESS

*Naga tribesmen in their traditional costume of colourfully-woven robes
with red sash, and headwear decorated with horns, black fur and
feathers. Elders of the tribe wear chin-straps decorated with animal
claws and the women wear colourful beads and decorate their faces with
geometrical tatoos.*

189

FEARSOME REPUTATION

*'Having a few gangs of Nagas working in the district was always
rather amusing…the local Burmese made no effort to hide their fear of
them, much to the amusement of the Nagas. They had nothing to
fear…there was no written contract, but I never knew a Naga who did
not keep his word completely.'*
A A Lawson, Life in the Burmese Jungle *(1983)*

PADAUNG BEAUTY

Every year, from the age of five or six, the Padaung girl traditionally adds new rings to her collection, until she marries, by which time her neck should be physically elongated.

CHANGING WAYS

'There are people in this country called Padaungs who admire long necks in women. The girls wear broad brass rings to stretch their necks, and they put on more and more of them until in the end they have necks like giraffes. It's no queerer than bustles or crinolines.'
George Orwell, Burmese Days *(1934)*

A DAY'S WORK

'Rings worn on arms and legs may weigh a woman down with an additional 30 pounds of brass. Since leg coils hamper walking, the women waddle…After years of being straightjacketed in brass, the neck muscles atrophy. If the rings are cut off, a brace must support the neck until exercises rebuild the muscles.'

John Keshishian, Anatomy of a Burmese Beauty Secret, National Geographic *(June 1979)*

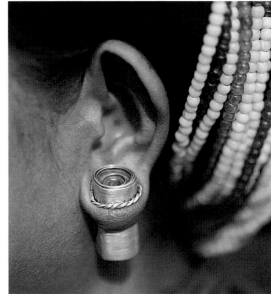

BAUBLES, BANGLES AND BEADS

Women of the Palaung tribe wear silver bangles around the waist and wrists and heavy silver studs in their ears. This conspicuous jewellery is a sign of their social status and wealth.

A FLEETING THOUGHT

*The Palaung are descendants of Mon-Khmer stock and are famous
for growing tea. Their traditional dress is very colourful; the women
wear white, green, pink, red and blue jackets over a distinctive
red-striped longyi and an ornate headdress of twisted beads.*

196

SHAN MARKET AT MAYMYO

*The Shan were the first immigrants to the northern states. Descended
from Tai-Chinese stock, they are traditionally traders but are also
well known for their silverware and lacquerware.*

MORNING MARKET, MYITKYINA

*Myitkyina – which means 'near the big river' – is the capital of
Kachin State. The region's markets boast the finest range of fruit and
vegetables in Myanmar.*

CEREMONIAL BEST

Strips of coloured cloth and coins are sewn onto the elaborate Akha
headdress and a brightly-woven jacket is worn over embroidered
leggings and dress. A young Kachin girl shows off a colourful hood
decorated with strings of pom-poms.

STANDING OUT IN A CROWD
A Chin girl displays her traditional black turban and dress inset with strips of brightly-woven cloth.

200

HIMALAYAN BORDERLAND

Myanmar's northern borders are high in the remote Himalayan region, which is partly a continuation of China's Yunnan plateau. Myanmar's highest peak – Hkakabo Razi (5,881 m) – overlooks east Tibet.

CHAPTER EIGHT

LU~MYO BAUNG~ZON

Portraits of Life

By Norman Lewis

*'[Myanmar has]…an **atmosphere** – a something undefined which has appealed irresistibly to all who have fallen under its influence. The appeal lies no doubt in the happy gaiety of the people, the kindly tolerance of their customs…and their grace. A kindly indolence lingers amidst the fretful restlessness of our age…They are attractive people, gay, humorous and often intellectual…little spoiled by the abominable spirit of our times.'*

203

C M Enriques, A Burmese Wonderland *(1922)*

The driver of a three-wheel taxi patiently awaits his next customer.

204

The golden Buddha looks down on novice monks, Mandalay Hill.

I AM PROBABLY ONE OF THE FEW persons to have been tipped by a taxi driver. It was a small matter, yet provided an unforgettable moment of illumination of a cultural and spiritual divide between the East, as represented by Burma, and the West. The driver, affectionately known locally as Oh-oh, charged reasonable sums for ferrying Burmese passengers in his canary-coloured taxi about the southern town of Moulmein, but offered his services free to foreigners deposited there for a day or two when the ship from Rangoon put into port. Most of these fares, Oh-oh had heard, were enjoying a temporary escape from the capital where visits into the surrounding countryside were not permitted. Like so many of his countrymen he was constantly on the alert for an opportunity to acquire merit. Being kind to foreigners came under the heading of meritorious actions.

When the *Menam* tied up, the yellow jeep would be seen waiting on the quay with Oh-oh offering a free ride to the new arrivals to any part of the town plus a visit to the pagoda at Mudon, a few miles away, if the road happened to be clear of insurgents.

At the end of such trips passengers received a small present in the form of an ornament cut from mother-of-pearl. In my case the gift was a superior-quality bird's nest. We had visited the caves where the earliest of the season's nests were being collected, and this was the first 'number one' nest of that day. It had probably been finished only the day before and was therefore spotlessly clean – a tiny amber saucer constructed from secretions in glands located in the bird's head. The collector gained merit too by giving it away, and we shook hands and he congratulated me with a wide smile when Oh-oh passed it over.

Oh-oh now proposed that we should take breakfast – it was by this time midday – by joining a party given by a local family to celebrate the entry of their son into the Buddhist noviciate. We found ourselves in a large hall-like room in which we joined about 200 people seated upon mats on a polished floor. Oh-oh assured me that our host had collected many of the guests at random off the streets.

Girls dressed in old-style finery were going round distributing snacks of pickled tea-leaves, salted ginger and shredded prawns. Once again merit-gain was what mattered and it was an occasion for the family to give a substantial portion of their possessions away. However, it might take them two years, Oh-oh thought, to settle the debts incurred by this entertainment.

It was Oh-oh who warned me, when I told him of my hope to travel in the interior of the country, that I should do something to modify the extreme pallor of my skin. 'They will not stare because they are polite', he said, 'but the young people in the villages have never seen an Englishman before.'

'What can I do about it?'

'You may make your face darker by keeping it as much as you can in the sun.'

I took this warning seriously and after three days' exposure on the deck of the *Menam* my skin was the colour of freshly-cut mahogany, except for white circles left by the sunglasses round the eyes. This caused some amusement among the European passengers, but evoked the sympathetic concern of the Burmese, one of whom being the assistant purser who confided in me his belief that I was the victim of witchcraft.

There was no outright prohibition on foreigners travelling in the interior of Burma at this time, six years after the conclusion of World War II, but those who arrived in Rangoon found that such were the obstacles encountered in their efforts to do so that they soon gave up. When I presented my letter of introduction to U Thant, head of the Ministry of Information, he saw no reason why I should not go where I wished. Later he admitted that this being his first experience of a request to travel in the country he was not sure of the official procedure to be followed. I was to be informed afterwards too that the US military attaché had fared no better and that a team sent over by *LIFE* magazine to do a picture reportage had, in the end, left the country after two uninteresting weeks spent in the famous Strand Hotel, Rangoon.

In the early morning locals visit the markets in Lashio near to China.

The days slipped away while I was passed from office to office, handled always with wonderful courtesy, encouraged in my hopes and commiserated with upon my many frustrations.

Escape was by the greatest of flukes. Someone told me that a certain powerful general was the only person that could do anything for me. I was admitted to his office to be received by a man overflowing with charm. My face was by this time covered in blisters but whatever surprise he may have felt at this spectacle nothing of it showed. The fluke consisted in his occupation at the moment of my arrival with the translation of a recently issued British military manual into Burmese, and the difficulties he had run into, for although he had been at Sandhurst, certain of the terms employed had since then been changed. 'Happen to know anything about this kind of thing?' he asked and amazingly enough I did. One hour later I left his presence with the pass in my pocket that was open sesame to any part of Burma. 'Damn interesting trip, I should imagine', he said. 'Won't find it too comfortable, but have a great time.'

The question was where, and how, to travel at a time when the Burmese army was at grips with five different brands of insurgents in the provinces and the small town of Syriam, just across the river from Rangoon, was under attack by dacoits. The disruptions of war had left a gap of a dozen miles in the main line connecting Rangoon with the old capital, Mandalay, and steamers using the Irrawaddy to carry goods and passengers up-country were sometimes cannonaded. Travelling rough could still be undertaken on traders' lorries, generally supposed to have come to an arrangement with insurgent bands, but there was nowhere in the interior to stay, not even a single hotel, and the *dak* bungalows, providing rough accommodation in the past, were closed or had been destroyed.

Happily Mandalay could still be reached by plane, and two days later I landed there to be met by Mr Tok Gale of the British Information Service, who told me that he had arranged for me to sleep in the projection room of the town's only cinema and would do his best to find a seat for me on a lorry going north. I was astounded to hear that he lived in what was officially described as the town's dacoit zone two miles away.

Tok Gale instructed me in the protocol of travel by Burmese lorry. Drivers, he said, did not accept money, but it was in order to be presented with small gifts and he suggested that I should carry such items as key-rings and plastic combs. Postcards of the coronation of George VI were also eagerly collected, and he had brought along a selection of these. 'You will be seated next to the driver', he

Tea shop, Shan State. In Myanmar, green tea is drunk with every meal.

said. 'Please take trouble to compliment him on his driving skills whenever occasion arises.' There was a word of warning: 'Beware in conversation of disparaging dacoits. These persons may be respectably dressed and mingling unobserved with lawful passengers.'

The journey to Mandalay went off without incident, but on the night of my arrival, while walking in the deserted main street, I was attacked by a pariah dog that bit me calmly and quietly in the calf before strolling away. Fortunately the only place of business open was a bar where I bought a bottle of Fire Tank brand Mandalay Whisky to disinfect the wound. I increased my popularity on the next leg of the trip by sharing the remainder of this with such of my companions who were not subjected to a religious fast. From this experience I learned the usefulness of religious fasts when rejecting unappetising food such as lizards in black sauce served in roadside stalls in the north.

The first stretch of the journey was to Myitkyina, where the road came to an end in the north, followed by a route virtually encircling the north-east through Bhamo, Wanting – almost within sight of China – Lashio, then weeks later back to Mandalay. At Bhamo you could pick up beautiful pieces of jade for next to nothing and, to my huge delight, a circuit house for travelling officials (although there were none) was actually open, directed by a butler straight out of the Victorian epoch who addressed me as 'honoured Sir', instantly provided tea with eggs lightly boiled and later a bed with sheets.

A final adventure was protective custody into which I was taken in the small town of Mu-Sé. Once again I slept contentedly, this time in a police station, and by day was accompanied on pleasant country walks by a heavily-armed policeman, who was as much interested as I in wildlife and natural history.

Thereafter all was plain sailing. Children had long since ceased to be alarmed by my ravaged features and pariah dogs were no longer perturbed by an alien smell. At Bhamo again I took the river steamer down the Irrawaddy to Mandalay, 'a pleasure-making excursion' as the man who sold the tickets described it, and he was absolutely right. For three days we chugged softly through these delectable riverine scenes. We were entertained by a professional storyteller, musicians strummed on archaic instruments, and once in a while the girls put on old-fashioned costumes to perform a spirited dance. There was a single moment of drama that was less alarming than theatrical. Insurgents hidden in the dense underbrush at the water's edge fired a few shots. Those on deck took momentary refuge behind bales of malodorous fish piled there.

No one was hurt and by the time I arrived on the scene from below, our military escort, who had blasted away at nothing in particular, had put down their guns and gone back to their gambling.

Next day Tok Gale welcomed me back in Mandalay. 'No complications with journey, I am hoping? No bad effects from meeting with dog?'

'None at all. Everything went off perfectly. Couldn't have been better.'

'I am relieved. Well at least something will be done now about all those dogs on our streets.'

'So, you're actually getting rid of them then?' I asked.

'For a while, yes. Abbot U Thein San is taking them into his pagoda compound for feeding and smarten up. They will be released in a better frame of mind. It is belief they will give no more trouble. In Mandalay we are used to seeing them. We should be regretful to miss their presence.'

'It's to be understood', I said.

'So how are you planning return to Rangoon?'

'I'm taking the train.'

Tok Gale seemed doubtful about this. 'For train travel they are saying that things are worse than they were. Rangoon train never arrives at destination.'

'I've been hearing that so I took the precaution of having a horoscope done at the stupa of King Pyu Sawhti.'

'Ah yes. This is famous monarch hatched from egg. And was result satisfactory?'

'Entirely so. The *ponggyi* told me I was good for another 30 years.'

Consulting a palm-reader or astrologer is a common practice in Myanmar.

'Well, that is splendid omen', Tok Gale said. 'So 6.15 to Rangoon is holding few terrors for you?'

'How can it after a horoscope like that?'

Tok Gale laughed and shook his head in mock reproach. 'Now I must tell you something, Mr Lewis. You are falling into our ways.'

NORMAN LEWIS *is one of the world's most acclaimed travel writers. His books include 'The Sicilian Specialist', 'A Dragon Apparent' and 'Golden Earth', a richly evocative account of his travels in Burma in 1950.*

Passengers all get off to help push a broken-down train along the railway track.

WATCHING THE WORLD GO BY
'The Burman is easy going, casual and satisfied with a little.'
W R Winston (1892).

AN AVID READER
Myanmar is a nation of readers. This old man, in his eighties, is
oblivious to onlookers.

THE CHINESE INFLUENCE
*Myanmar's Chinese settlers are descendants of merchants who settled
on trade routes along the great rivers.*

KING OF THE ROAD
*The bicycle is the most popular form of transport in towns and villages
throughout Myanmar.*

GENTLE BEAUTY
'There is something gentle and flower-like about Burmese women.
The gentleness comes from within; the flower quality in their
physical make-up.'
Ira J Morris, My East Was Gorgeous *(1958)*

CHILDHOOD AND OLD AGE
Children are treated with great kindness in Myanmar where fathers
and grandparents take an active role in their upbringing.

JOURNEY'S END

'In old age…his [the Burman's] manners become gentle and reserved,
his face catches a spiritual expression.'
V C Scott O'Connor, The Silken East *(1904)*

NEW BEGINNING

'Babies [in Burma]… grow up little merry things…very sedate, very
humorous, very rarely crying.'
H Fielding, The Soul of a People *(1899)*

216

ON GUARD

*At the entrance to a village hut in Haka, the capital of Chin State, the
Reverend Van Hre, a Haka Chin priest, wears traditional dress.*

AT YOUR SERVICE

Stewards on an Ayeyarwaddy River steamer welcome passengers aboard. The journey between Yangon and Mandalay is always busy.

WOMEN'S WORK

'The bazaar is almost wholly run by women, each having her own stall and keeping the accounts in her head. Vastly better than her indolent husband or brother, she knows how to make money and keep what she makes.'

H P Cochrane, Amongst the Burmans *(1904)*

221

FREE TO TRADE

*'In Burma, she [the woman] has had to look out for herself: she has
had the freedom to come to grief as well as... strength.'*
H Fielding, The Soul of a People *(1899)*

BEAUTY OF YOUTH
'Her cheek is more beautiful than the dawn,
Her eyes deeper than river pools'
Burmese love song

OLD AGE
'Thin hair, fallen teeth, wrinkled skin and dim eyes augur the season
of destruction.'
Ngwe Ta Yi, Old Age Joy *(1953)*

224

TIME TO SPARE

'He [the Burman] does not need to earn his bread with the sweat of his brow…when his patch of paddy land has been reaped, his only concern is how to pass the time, and that is no difficult matter where he had plenty of cheroots and betel-nut.'
Shway Yoe, The Burman, His Life and Notions *(1882)*

LIFE'S CYCLE
*'Old age brings with it a wonderful change [for the Burman]…the
growth within him of spiritual desire.'*
V C Scott O'Connor, The Silken East *(1904)*

MOTHER AND CHILD
*'Great love and indulgence is given to Burmese children, who are
considered very precious.'*
Mi Mi Khaing, World of Burmese Women *(1984)*

ACKNOWLEDGEMENTS

Co & Bear Productions Ltd would like to extend their thanks to all the people and organisations
mentioned throughout this volume and to the following:

Ministry of Information, Yangon

Ministry of Tourism, Yangon

Yangon Enterprises

Department of Human Settlement and Housing Development, Yangon

Yangon City Development Committee

Orbis Publishing Ltd, London, England

Istituto Geografico De Agostini, Novara, Italy

SELECT BIBLIOGRAPHY

Aung-Thwin, M, Pagan, The Origins of Modern Burma, *University of Hawaii Press (1985)*

Bixler, N, Burmese Journey, *The Antioch Press (1967)*

Bryce, J, Burma: the Country and People, *Royal Geographical Society (1886)*

Byles, M, Journey into Buddhist Silence, *George Allen & Unwin Ltd (1962)*

Cochrane, H P, Amongst the Burmans, *Fleming H Revell & Co (1904)*

Collis, M, Siamese White, *Faber and Faber (1951)*

Cuming, E, In the Shadow of the Pagoda: Sketches of Burmese Life and Character, *W H Allen (1897)*

Dingwall, A (ed), Traveller's Literary Companion to South-east Asia, *In Print Publishing (1994)*

Enriques, C M, A Burmese Wonderland, *Thatcher, Spink & Co (1922)*

Fielding, H, The Soul of a People, *Macmillan & Co (1899)*

Fraser-Lu, S, Burmese Crafts Past and Present, *Oxford University Press (1994)*

Fytche, A, Burma, Past and Present, *C Kegan Paul & Co (1925)*

Gascoigne, G, Among Pagodas and Fair Ladies: An account of a tour through Burma, *A D Innes & Co (1896)*

Griswold A et al, Art of the World: Burma, Korea, Tibet, *Methuen (1964)*

Harcourt Robinson, C, Burmese Vignettes, *Luzac & Co. Ltd (1949)*

Harris, W, East for Pleasure, *Edward Arnold (1929)*

Harvey, G, History of Burma, *Longmans, Green & Co (1925)*

Hla Pe, Burmese Proverbs, *John Murray (1962)*

Judson, E, Life of Adironam Judson, *Anson D F Randolph & Co (1883)*

Khaing, M M, Burmese Family, *Longmans, Green & Co (1946)*

Khaing, M M, The World of Burmese Women, *Zed Books Ltd. (1984)*

Khin Myo Chit, A Wonderland of Burmese Legends, *The Tamarind Press (1984)*

Khin Myo Chit, Gift of Laughter *(1995)*

Kingdon-Ward, F, Return to the Irrawaddy, *Andrew Melrose (1956)*

Kipling, R, Selected Poems, *Penguin (1993)*

Lawson, A A, Life in the Burmese Jungle, *Sussex: The Book Guild (1983)*

Lewis, N, Golden Earth, *Jonathan Cape (1952)*

Ma Ma Lay, Not out of Hate *(trs. Margaret Aung-Thwin), Ohio University Center for International Studies (1991)*

Marshall, Rev H I, The Karen People of Burma, *University of Columbia Press (1922)*

Ma Thanegi, The Illusion of Life: Burmese Marionettes, *White Orchid Press (1994)*

Maugham, W S, The Gentleman in the Parlour, *William Heinemann (1930)*

Maung Htin Aung, Folk Elements in Burmese Buddhism *(1959)*

Maung Htin Aung, A History of Burma, *Columbia University Press (1967)*

Morris, I J, My East was Gorgeous, *Hutchinson & Co (1958)*

O'Connor, V C Scott, The Silken East, *Hutchinson & Co (1904)*

Orwell, G, Burmese Days, *Penguin (1989)*

Pe Maung Tin & G H Luce, The Glass Palace Chronicles of the Kings of Burma, *Oxford University Press (1923)*

Rodrigue, Y, Nat-Pwe, Burma's Supernatural Sub-culture, *Kiscadale (1992)*

Sao Htun Hmat Win, The Initiation of Novicehood and the Ordination of Monkhood
in the Burmese Buddhist Culture, *Dept of Religious Affairs, Yangon (1986)*

Scott, Sir J G, Burma, A Handbook of Practical Information, *David O'Connor (1921)*

Stanford, J, Far Ridges: A Record of Travel in North-Eastern Burma 1938-39, *C & J Temple (1944)*

Shway Yoe, The Burman, His Life and Notions, *Macmillan & Co (1882)*

U Tok Gale, Burmese Timber Elephant, *Trade Corporation, Yangon (1974)*

Wheeler, J T, Journal of a Voyage up the Irrawaddy, *J W Baynes (1871)*

Wiggins, M, John Dollar, *Penguin (1989)*

Williams, Lt-Col J H, Elephant Bill, *Rupert Hart-Davis (1950)*

SILVER SPONSORS

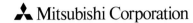

FUJIFILM PHOTO FILM PTE LTD

Fujifilm was founded in 1934 with its headquarters in Tokyo. Presently it has more than 30 offices worldwide.

The company manufactures, markets and distributes amateur and professional colour films, papers, photographic equipment, cameras, X-ray films, graphic arts films, PS plates and equipment, cinematographic films, audio and video tapes.

MITSUBISHI CORPORATION

Mitsubishi Corporation is one of Japan's leading general trading companies with 232 offices in 87 countries employing 14,000 people.

Drawing on its considerable expertise in the fields of information, financing, investment and organisation, Mitsubishi Corporation is looking at increasing the exports of Myanma goods.

MYANMA SILVER AND RUBY CO LTD

Myanma Silver and Ruby Co Ltd, part of the KLN Group, is the first private official gem and jewellery company in Myanmar. It supplies gems and stones to the international market as well as supplying shops and private clients in Myanmar with the best in gems, jewellery and silverwares.

SHANGRI–LA HOTELS AND RESORTS

Internationally renowned for spacious guest rooms and excellent standards of service and facilities, Shangri-La's hotels and resorts welcome you throughout Asia Pacific. The new hotels for quality business-class accommodation, *Traders*, also offer our legendary warmth and charm. Visit the new Traders Hotel in Yangon and enjoy Asian hospitality at its best.

SILKAIR

In 1992 Silkair was transformed from a holiday resort airline to a fully-fledged regional operator, catering for both business and leisure passengers. Silkair continues to work hand in hand with its parent company, Singapore Airlines, focusing on new Asian destinations and regional connections, with business passengers particularly well catered for.

Summit Parkview
Yangon

SUMMIT PARKVIEW, YANGON

Owned by a partnership of Singapore companies Summit Parkview is Yangon's first international hotel for business travellers. With 250 guest rooms and suites, a modern business centre, banquet facilities, fitness centre and pool, hair and beauty salon, clinic, shops, restaurants and entertainment, it also offers a business-like approach and international telecommunications.

GOLD SPONSORS

KAINNARIE

KAINNARIE PROPERTY HOLDINGS LTD

Kainnarie Property Holdings Ltd was formed to identify an enduring niche in property development and related businesses, and to constructively engage its resources in offering products that would be beneficial to its customers.

The company aims to respond, in collaboration with foreign input, to the fast-changing economic scenario by forming prudent goals in the best interests of the customers. Its mission is to ensure customer satisfaction.

Involving the resources of businesses already established in Myanmar, the company has the necessary expertise to kick off its activities. KPH is resolute in its mission to develop businesses that shall be most beneficial to the people of Myanmar as a whole.

MPL PTE LTD

The present MPL group of companies was formed from the amalgamation of two holding companies, MPL Pte Ltd and SIM LIM Co (Myanmar) Ltd. The MPL Group has been operating in Myanmar since 1989 and, with over 120 staff, the Group has three Strategic Business Units: Trading, Engineering and Export.

The Trading Business Unit's main sphere of activity evolves around the supply of Nippon Paint, waterproofing products, general trading and property development. The Engineering Business Unit focuses mainly on the building services arena, and provides services in the area of M & E Interior Design and M & E supplies. The Export Business Unit deals solely in the export of seafood and commodities.

The Group objective is to play a humble but vital part in contributing to a better Myanmar.

PT PRIMA COMEXINDO

Established in 1986 Prima Comexindo has the privilege of being recognised as Indonesia's premier trading house with an established reputation as a specialist in the implementation of trade between developing countries. We have established a network of offices around the world and important commercial and political relationships spanning the globe.

Although Myanmar is a recent market it is a fast-growing one – a major supplier of beans, rice and fishery products with an expanding market for building materials. With our branch office in Yangon established in 1993, we are actively promoting investment in Myanmar's infrastructure and in its resource-based industries.

SEDONA HOTELS INTERNATIONAL

Sedona Hotels International is a dynamic hotel management and development company officially launched in Singapore in 1994. It is one of the first Singapore-based hotel management companies to export Singaporean expertise overseas.

The company's mission is simple – to create a hotel experience that makes Sedona a distinctive choice for travellers on business or leisure.

In 1992 Straits Hotels and Resorts, under the Keppel Corporation of Singapore, was set up to develop a fully-fledged hotel management company. Sedona Hotels International now manages hotels in Yangon and Mandalay in Myanmar as well as hotels and resorts in south-east Asia, China and Australia.

SERGE PUN & ASSOCIATES (MYANMAR) LTD

Serge Pun & Associates (Myanmar) Ltd, known as SPAM, began investing in Myanmar in 1990. Since then SPAM has assumed a leadership role in economic development in Myanmar and achieved international recognition for a sizeable and successful investment portfolio and the ability to attract and efficiently service foreign investors. Financial and organisational depth provides the ability to source and respond to attractive investment opportunities.

SPAM promotes and manages successful private and public companies and investment syndications. Projects include real estate, banking and finance, industry, hospitality and services, trading, infrastructure and consulting. All offer investors the same assurance of superior return on investment.

CONTRIBUTING PHOTOGRAPHERS

MICHAEL FREEMAN has written 23 books on photography. His photographs have recently been published in the book *Palaces of the Gods*.

ZAW MIN YU is from Burma originally and now lives in Sydney. He contributes to *Geo* Australia, and held his first solo exhibition on Myanmar in Sydney last year. He also works for corporations on assignments, including Saatchi and Saatchi, McCann-Ericksonn and Leo Burnett.

TIM HALL specialises in Asia and has been involved in books on Cambodia, Vietnam, Hong Kong and Laos.

BARRY BROMAN lives in Yangon, where he is the American Foreign Service Officer for the United States Embassy. He is a specialist on South East Asia, has contributed to magazines such as Architectural Digest, and has worked for Associated Press in Thailand as its official photographer.

STEVE MCCURRY is the top photographer for the *National Geographic*. His pictures of Myanmar were published in the July 1995 issue.

CHRIS STEELE-PERKINS is half Burmese and was born in Rangoon. He just recently returned to Myanmar and is one of the most well-known travel photographers, represented by the Magnum agency.

BRUNO BARBEY contributes to *National Geographic*, and is represented by the Magnum agency.

PHOTOGRAPHY

Michael Freeman 7,12BR,12TR,24,28L,28BR,34,35,43,45BL,47R,49,60,68,72,122,128,129,143,144,146,147, 148L,148R,149,176,177,178T,181,182,183,184,185TL,185BL,185R,194L,194R,197,202,203,204B,205,206, 211,213.

Tim Hall 6T,6B,8,11,14,15,22,23TL,23R,25,26,27,29,30,31,32BR,36TR,36BR,37,38,39,40B,41,42,44,45TL, 47L,48,50,53,63,64R,66,67,69,70,71,74,75,80,82,83,86L,86R,87,90L,90R,91,92,93,94,96L,96R,97,99,100, 101,126,130L,130R,131,136R,137,145T,150,153,158,160,179,180,187,188TR,188BR,189,196,204T,210,212, 214,217,218,219,224,225,226, END PAPERS.

Barry Broman 9,10L,13,17,23BL,36L,45R,46,51TL,51BL,58,59,62,77,102R,106,107,108,109,110,111,112,113L, 113R,114L,114TR,114BR,115,116,117,118,119,120T,120B,121,123,124L,124R,125,132,133,134L,134TR, 134BR,135,136L,139,142T,142B,145B,152,157,159,161,164B,165,166,167,174,175,188L,195,198L,198R, 199,207T,220,221,222,223.

Zaw Min Yu FRONT COVER 10TR,10BR,12L,19,28TR,32TR,32L,33,40T,52BR,54,55,56,57,61,64L,73,76B,78, 79,81,84,85,88,89,95,98,102L,103,127R,156,178B,190,191,192,208,209,215,227.

Steve McCurry 4,5,20,21,76T,104,105,162,163,173.

Chris Steele-Perkins 18,138,140,141,154,155,193,207B.

Richard Gayer 164T,168,169,170,171L,171R,172.

Htein Win 16L,16TR,16BR,52L,52TR,127L,186,216.

Bruno Barney 151. *John Cleare* 200,201. *T.Hopker* 51R. *Hiroji Kubota* 65.

Map Illustration by Andrew Farmer.